S0-BTA-169

# Moving Up to Supervision

## SECOND EDITION

Martin M. Broadwell
Cartoons by Johnny Sajem

A Wiley-Interscience Publication

John Wiley & Sons
New York / Chichester / Brisbane / Toronto / Singapore

Copyright © 1986 by John Wiley & Sons, Inc.

All rights reserved. Published simultaneously in Canada.

Reproduction or translation of any part of this work
beyond that permitted by Section 107 or 108 of the
1976 United States Copyright Act without the permission
of the copyright owner is unlawful. Requests for
permission or further information should be addressed to
the Permissions Department, John Wiley & Sons, Inc.

This publication is designed to provide accurate and
authoritative information in regard to the subject
matter covered. It is sold with the understanding that
the publisher is not engaged in rendering legal, accounting,
or other professional service. If legal advice or other
expert assistance is required, the services of a competent
professional person should be sought. *From a Declaration
of Principles jointly adopted by a Committee of the
American Bar Association and a Committee of Publishers.*

**Library of Congress Cataloging-in-Publication Data:**

Broadwell, Martin M.
   Moving up to supervision.

   (Wiley series in training and development)
   Includes index.
   1. Supervision of employees. I. Title. II. Series.

HF5549.B854   1986        658.3′02        85-29411
ISBN 0-471-83677-X

Printed in the United States of America

10 9 8 7 6 5 4 3 2

To all those bottom-of-the-ladder
supervisors, all over the world,
who carry the brunt of the
production responsibility on their
shoulders, this book is humbly
dedicated.

# Preface

Once when I had just finished a week-long training program for new supervisors, a young, nonsupervising engineer came up to me with an urgent request. He had wangled his way into the class, though he was not then a supervisor nor had he immediate hopes of becoming one. However, he had a strong desire to someday become one, and it was to this end he aired his request. "Why doesn't somebody write a book for the *aspiring* supervisor? I would like very much to become a supervisor, and I read all the books about what to do *after* I am one, but they don't help me now. I don't have anyone to practice delegation on; I don't do any appraisals; I don't have anyone to train. How can I learn enough to be at least looked at for promotion?" From this plea came this book. Within the next week I had outlined it, and shortly after finished it. It became my challenge and my fetish; write something to help people become supervisors that will allow them to learn and practice, when they apparently have no one to practice on. I hope I've accomplished this.

For the few who have used this book it has served them

well, both for presupervisory training and new supervisory work. Unfortunately the first edition was published by a lesser known publisher, one who had interests in fields other than human resource development. As a result the book did not have wide distribution. When the opportunity arose to have a well-known publisher edit and reissue the book under their label, it was an exciting moment. The second edition is essentially the same as the previously published book, with two major additions. The first came at the suggestion of earlier readers, namely to add thought and discussion questions at the end of each chapter. The aim of these questions is primarily to stimulate the reader to review the content in more detail. These questions will also help the classroom instructor when there is need for discussion in a training session. The second major addition is a new chapter entitled, "Things employees don't like about supervisors." This chapter came about as a result of asking hundreds of employees questions about things that bosses do that irritate, displease, or make them angry. The list is longer than that included here, but these are the things most often cited.

The author wishes the best of supervision to all those who have made it, and those who aspire to it!

MARTIN M. BROADWELL

*Decatur, Georgia*
*April 1986*

# Preface to the First Edition

There are many people in the work world who have the potential to become supervisors. Many of them eventually do become supervisors, and many of these become good ones. For the most part, they are poorly prepared for the job when they get it. Often, it's a matter of finding out on Friday that they will be supervisors on Monday. When that happens no amount of cramming will prepare them for the task awaiting them on Monday. This book has several objectives:

1. To provide some advance help for those who will find out on the spur of the moment that they've just been promoted
2. To provide help for those who have potential but don't know how to utilize it
3. To provide assistance in training those who are aware of their move to supervision but have time for some pre-supervisory training

These, we think, are worthwhile goals.

The reader should bear in mind that the more he or she

knows about supervision ahead of time the easier the job will be when it comes. Not all the skills needed by a supervisor are explained in this book. Mostly, we've talked about the "survival" skills, the things that are needed on that fateful Monday morning. Much time has been spent in trying to show how the person aspiring to supervision can work—on the present assignment—to find out just what skills he or she presently has, and what can be done along the way to overcome the shortcomings.

We've tried to show how management thinks when it comes to promoting people, and what we can do to fit into this thinking. Nowhere have we suggested that it is all a game, and that by doing certain subtle things, we can outsmart management and be chosen over others. What we have tried to do is to make it clear that for the most part, we control our own destiny. We can make our own luck, as we'll see in the last chapter. We've tried to show an alternative to just being a mediocre employee. Above all, we've offered an opportunity for the reader to try to do things that should lead to becoming a supervisor. It's not a simple formula, but the points given for the person wanting to move up to supervision are tested and they've withstood the test. They not only have worked for those who've made it to supervision, but they'll work for any of us who is willing to work doing the right things to get there.

MARTIN M. BROADWELL

*Decatur, Georgia*
*1978*

# Acknowledgments

In my years of working, I've had some bad supervisors. They've helped me, though, for the good ones showed up in much marked contrast. Taken on the average, I'd have to say that the supervisors were probably better as supervisors than I was as an employee under them. For all of them I'm deeply grateful. I'll not name the bad ones, nor all the good ones, but I would like to offer a special "Thanks!" to the following people who have at one time or another been responsible for me and my work efforts. They've made a better person out of me because of their supervision:

Wailes Thomas
W. L. ("Bill") Sullivan
W. C. ("Zeb") Burnett
Leise G. Robbins
J. Harley Waldron

M.M.B.

# Prologue

Supervision is an integral part of the free enterprise system, which in turn is a competitive system. For that reason, supervision is in many ways a competitive arrangement, where there is competition to get there and competition to perform as well as others in the supervisory role. Unless this competition causes too much conflict or produces less than satisfactory results, it is a good situation. Quality should never fear competition, so good supervisors should never fear to get into competitive situations, unless there is a lack of confidence in the ability to perform. Frequently, this is exactly what happens to those who aspire to be supervisors: They wonder about their ability to perform as required to meet the challenge of the job. This book is aimed at helping to instill that confidence and offers skills that will enable the aspirant to be able to meet that challenge.

Supervision differs from nonsupervisory functions in the organization in one major way. It is a matter of getting the job done through others. It is not merely the difference between white and blue collar workers, between managing and nonmanaging, or between levels in the organization.

The difference is essentially a matter of who does the work. In nonsupervisory jobs, the person assigned the task does the work; he or she does not delegate it to another. In supervisory jobs, there are those who have the responsibility of doing the work and those who have the responsibility of seeing that the work gets done. The latter job is that of the supervisor.

The supervisory role is neither as good as it sounds to those who aspire to it, nor as bad as it sounds from those who complain about being a supervisor. Supervisors are neither magicians nor saints . . . just essential elements in getting the job done well.

# Contents

# Moving Up
## to Supervision

## chapter one

# The Role of the Supervisor in the Organization

When people aspire to become supervisors, they may do it for several reasons. It may be that they think the supervisor's job is an easy one, and they'd like to have some of that leisure time supervisors seem to have. Then again, they may decide that the pay is high and what better motivation is there than that? (Actually, we'll see that there are better motivations, but the aspiring supervisor may not know them.) Some may want to be a supervisor because of the prestige, the power, the satisfaction, or the fulfillment of a "self-image." Maybe it's a combination of all these things. But whatever the reason for deciding to try to go the supervisor route, very few people take the job for the first time with a clear understanding of what a supervisor really does for a living. In this chapter, we'll provide a definition and describe the duties of a supervisor—any supervisor.

# THE PHILOSOPHY OF SUPERVISION

While many think the supervisor's role is unique in the organization, they rarely realize what it is that makes the role unique. When you get right down to it, there's only one thing that makes the supervisor's job different from others in the organization. It's not accountability, since every worker is accountable for his or her actions. It's not decision making or problem solving, since everybody in the organization has to make decisions and solve problems—from the lowest paid hourly worker to the highest paid and most educated *non-supervisor* research scientist. It's not the need for communications skills since every employee needs them to a certain degree—*some more than the supervisor* (those in contact with customers or those in hazardous jobs giving reports or up-to-minute data on operations, etc.). What is it then? Is it something so nebulous that it escapes definition? No, it's so simple that we tend to overlook it. The thing that makes the supervisor's job different from anybody else's in the organization is that the supervisor *must get the work done through other people*! Only when the supervisor is doing this is the job being done correctly. There may be times when the supervisor may pitch in and help, but those should be rare and exceptional.

When we start thinking about the philosophy of management and styles of managing people, we have to think in terms of getting other people to do the work. We'll say this several times in this book: the biggest problem most people have when they come up through the ranks in the organization to the job of supervisor is that they have trouble separating themselves from being a "worker" and thinking of themselves as "supervisors of workers." Everything we'll talk about in this book will relate to the relationship the supervisor has with his or her people in getting the job done through them. If anything can help a new supervisor, it is the belief that the uniqueness of the job is the responsibility of getting tasks done on time, within the proper specifications of management in terms of money, materials and people, *all by directing others* rather than personally doing the work.

# FUNCTIONS OF MANAGEMENT

We will use the word "management" rather loosely in this book, sometimes making a distinction between management and supervision, but mostly referring to management as a part of the business different from nonmanagement or the hourly working group. This means that supervisors are a part of management, and in most organizations this holds true. However, in some organizations there is a distinction made between a manager and a supervisor, but when one looks at their own job there is actually little difference. One thing will be constant in this book: Anytime we refer to a *supervisor* we're talking about somebody who has employees under him or her.

It's important that we know the function of people at different levels in the management hierarchy. Frequently we hear the terms "middle management," "top management" or "higher management," we'll need to understand the role or function of each of these management levels. It's easy to divide management into lower, middle, and top management when we're talking about duties and responsibilities. There are specific, defined areas for each of these levels for the organization to run smoothly. Things go much better when people are performing their functions at the right level, and do not overlap.

Let's talk a little about the duties, responsibilities, and functions of the three levels we just mentioned. The duties of top and bottom levels of management are easier to define than middle management's, hence problems more often arise at this level than at any other in the organization. Basically, we say that the higher the level of management, the more time is spent on long-range planning, giving direction to the organization and working on problems that have to do with setting up the structure of the organization (such as who's going to be working for whom, how many people will be in the organization, and how many levels will be there; we usually call this function "organizing"). Lower down the ladder of levels we should find people concerning themselves with short-range problems, such as directing people and checking on how well the work is done. We give names to these functions. At top level we should find people doing "planning" and "organizing" while at the bottom level we find people "directing" and "controlling." This doesn't mean that *some* of this isn't done at each level; it just means that this is where most of the time has to be spent. The first level of supervision is at the bottom of the management level, and is concerned with directing and controlling. Directing people to do their jobs includes appraising, disciplining, motivating, and other skills, as we'll see later. Controlling is simply watching what is being done in relationship to what *should* be done. Are the expenditures within the budget? Will the work get done on time? Will we meet the specifications of the customer? Are the safety rules being followed? Obviously these are things that top management shouldn't be doing, and if they are, the organization will become bogged down in a hurry. At the same time, it isn't the role of the first line supervisor to be concerned about the long-range plans of the organization.

One obvious reason for this division of responsibility is that little or nothing can be done in the way of setting policy at this lower level or getting the money or people to meet long-range plans. Another reason is that higher management has more information than do the lower levels about the direction and the future expectations, as far as markets, money, raw materials, and desires of the directors of the business or organization. Admittedly the lower levels know more about what is going on *day to day* than does top management, but that's why it's this level that worries about the short-range planning instead of the long-range planning. That's why top management has to depend on the lower levels to make daily decisions or decisions that will affect the organization in the short run.

After we've said all of this about top and bottom levels of management, it becomes obvious that we've not said anything about *middle* management. Do they have a function, too? By all means, but not nearly as defined as the other two. Middle management has several functions or roles, *including all four that we've mentioned earlier*. They have problems of long-range planning (as well as short-range) but are more frequently working in the intermediate range of planning, such as special projects that may take a year or two to complete. They certainly have to worry about the structure of the organization beneath them and often have the job of hiring and structuring the organization according to designs of the top management. They have to consider budgets and deadlines and report the findings to higher management, along with recommendations. They have to be aware of the problems of supervising people, or directing. Problems that are not handled at the lower level come directly to them, and their job is to "defuse" the problem before it gets out of hand.

Here we really have a good definition of the role of middle management. They act as a buffer between top and bottom levels of management, acting in both directions. Top management has much decision making to do about policy and procedures. It is up to middle management to relay these policies and procedures to the lower levels where they will be carried out. Often middle management will have to put some "meat on the bones" of the decisions and policies, giving substance to the decisions, translating them into the real world of activity. This is their job. But that's not all. They must pass information upwards, too. They must watch the results, analyze them and then give top management enough information and suggestions to make accurate decisions. It is through the middle managers that the first line supervisors should go with recommendations for change. It is to the middle management that the first line supervisor should go to for information on policies and procedures. The middle management people are well named, since they often are *in the middle*. They must explain the policies to the lower levels of management in ways they in turn can explain and defend to their people, and they must interpret accurately the data they are passing up to the top levels so that nothing will get lost in the translation. Top management relies almost entirely on them to give good, accurate, up-to-date, complete, and unbiased information. If they get anything other than this, the organization will suffer accordingly.

## THE MANY SKILLS OF SUPERVISION

When one considers becoming a supervisor it is often frightening to learn of the many skills required—in the long run—to become successful. Many "turn back at the gate" when they see the things that are required of them. Supervising is a formidable job; it does take many skills. One has to do a lot of things that require learning instead of just using common sense or "doing what comes naturally." However, there is an out to this, so the would-be supervisor need not panic. Most of these skills aren't needed the first day or first month of the job, as we'll see in a moment. Only a few basic skills are needed to get started, and they can be learned easily enough while the others are acquired.

We should at least look at the skills required so the aspiring employee can see the scope of the job ahead. We've already mentioned the two important functions, *directing* and *controlling*. These aren't exactly skills in themselves but are the result of doing many different skills. For example, directing people requires being acceptable in the skill of *communicating*. Communicating is a definable, observable skill, as we'll see in a later chapter. It's getting information accurately *to* one or more people. It's also gathering information from one or more people with this same accuracy. It requires the skill of listening, too. Dealing with people also requires *perception*—perceiving how people are reacting and predicting how they will react under certain circumstances. This can be learned.

There is the skill of *problem solving*; there are specific steps in problems which will lead to sound solutions to even the most difficult problems. But it can be learned. Closely akin to this is *decision making* which is another skill with definite procedures that, if followed, will lead to good decisions, but if not, will lead to sloppy decisions and half-thoughtout actions that will create trouble for a long time to come.

There are other skills, too. There's the *interpersonal* skill of getting people to believe in their work and to be motivated to perform up to standard. There's the matter of *delegation*, the key to most successful supervisory efforts. Since the job is one of getting the work done by others, delegation is the most important skill in our relations with our subordinates. The person who wants to be a supervisor should make up his or her mind early that this is the one skill that will be studied constantly and perfected if at all possible. By the way, as we'll see in Chapter 7, there's more to delegating than just telling somebody to do the job. We have to worry about morale, attitudes, and teamwork, and if we don't delegate properly, all of these things can quickly suffer.

There is the skill of *appraising* our employees. If we are going to delegate, we need to know each employee's ability to determine who would best handle the work. Part of appraising is telling employees what we've found out and what we think about their performance; this introduces the skill of *interviewing*. But we interview or meet face-to-face with our employees at times other than during an appraisal interview. We sometimes find that we have to *discipline* them which is another skill we have to learn. Correcting employees who are not performing up to standard or who are breaking the rules in some way isn't an easy task, since here again, we must be concerned with the future of that employee's attitude, the morale of the group and the effect of the discipline on team effort in the future. But *not* disciplining is just as detrimental, so we have to learn the skill. Another kind of interviewing is *counseling*, a skill required when an employee has a personal problem or some problem that may not be directly job related but is interfering with the employee's performance—or may interfere if it's not corrected. Usually these interviews occur at the request of the employee, but we should be prepared when they do come up and that's another skill we have to learn.

Delegating and appraising introduce another need: the skill of *training*. If we are going to expect employees to accept the responsibilities we give them, and if they are going to be appraised on their performance, we owe it to the employees to see that they are trained to do that which we've delegated to them. *Training people is a skill.* It can and must be learned when one becomes a supervisor. As we'll see later, there is the danger that we *think* we know how to train, go through some motions called training, then put the blame on the employee when the job is done incorrectly. That's not fair to the employee and it's not very good supervision.

## THE SURVIVAL SKILLS

We could go on for several more pages discussing the many skills that will ultimately be needed by the supervisor, but this would only serve to discourage the reader, rather than to offer encouragement. Now we need to point out those skills that we will call "survival" skills because they are needed almost immediately on making supervisor. In fact, they can be worked on ahead of time, in anticipation of when we do make supervisor so we won't have to suffer any longer than necessary. Those new supervisors who have been successful in making it through the first several months without much trouble find that there are a few skills that will help them immediately while others can be acquired gradually without their suffering on the job.

We've already mentioned these skills along with others. They all have to do with getting the work done through others. In delegating work to others, we have to know *what* to delegate and what we can't delegate. We have to understand the difference between delegating authority, responsibility, and accountability. We have to understand that these are different things, and if we aren't careful we'll end up delegating too much, too little, or the wrong thing. Then there is the *way* we delegate, as we've already mentioned. There are right and wrong ways, and the person who wants to be successful at supervision has to do it properly.

Training is another of the survival skills. Training is often overlooked as a skill, but the people who look to supervision as a career need to put it in the proper perspective. It stands to reason that if we're going to have time to do all the things we need to do as a supervisor, we're going to need trained people under us. If we don't train them, who will? There are some specific steps in doing on-the-job training, and we'll look at these in detail later on. The aspiring supervisor should analyze his or her own training and decide what was good and bad about it, and what was the difference. Time is always a problem with supervisors, and efficiency in training is one way to save some time. Remember, it takes just as long to train people incorrectly as it does to train them correctly!

Another survival skill is the ability to recognize the talents and skills in our employees immediately. We may not be able to thoroughly analyze them or to know every talent they have, but we ought to be able to know how well they are doing the job we've given them to do. We get confused by a lot of things when we start to appraise our employees. Being new, we're likely to be impressed by the wrong things. We think about their attitudes toward us or the job or the assignments we give them, and substitute our opinion on these for facts about how they actually are doing on the job. One employee complains about being given a job, and we tend to see this employee as an unsatisfactory performer. Another employee is eager to take on the assignment and we are likely to rate that employee as a good performer. We may be wrong in both cases. We won't do a good job of appraising until we understand and learn the skill involved.

We learn very young not to like discipline. It's not at all unusual that most supervisors—new and old—fall down on the job most often when it comes to discipline. We don't like to do it, it's unpleasant, it stands to be threatening, and to make it worse, we really don't know how to do it very well. One resolution the would-be supervisor should make is that when an employee needs discipline, with the documenta-

"Atlee, I think I need to explain your supervisory role a little further before you start today."

tion there and with the evidence indicating the importance of doing it now *it will be done*! All the evidence we have about disciplining shows that there are many more regrets from not doing it than from doing it. There ought to be encouragement enough for us to learn the skill as soon as possible; not only learn it, but use it, too.

Every supervisor, *sooner than later*, will run into interpersonal conflict. It is present in every office, every plant, every work group at one time or another, to one degree or another. That it is undesirable does not diminish its existence one bit. Organizations are made up of people, and where there are people there will ultimately be conflict among them. We can reduce it, we can learn to live with it, we can ignore it, but we aren't likely to eliminate it. The successful supervisor must learn very soon after making supervisor how to deal with interpersonal conflict. To learn the causes is helpful in both dealing with it and preventing some of it; one also has to learn the best ways of handling it. A very fine, well-working organization can go sour very rapidly when conflict isn't handled quickly and expertly. For this reason, the skill of handling interpersonal conflict is included in the list of survival skills.

Throughout the common thread is "communicating." Each of the skills we've listed under the survival label is dependent a great deal on good communication. Earlier we described communcating, so here we'll add that it doesn't matter whether people are right or wrong if they can't communicate their decisions, thoughts, requests, or anxieties to other people. It doesn't matter whether it's delegating, appraising, training, disciplining, or handling interpersonal conflict, if we can't communicate (and that includes the ability to listen), we're not going to be able to do our job. All those reading this and expecting to become a supervisor someday should stop right now and think about the last time somebody misunderstood them: Whose fault was it?

Did we blame the other person? Did we try to correct *our* action or expect the other person to make the changes? Are we better at communicating than we were five years ago or are we staying the same or going backwards? These are legitimate questions and will have to be answered before there is consideration about becoming a successful supervisor. For what it's worth, we can be sure that those who will make the decisions on promoting us or not will answer these questions, whether we do or do not!

When we refer to survival skills, we wouldn't want to leave the impression that the other skills we mentioned or others that weren't mentioned are not important. To the contrary, they are important, and if we're going to be successful in the long run we'll have to learn all of them to some degree. The ones we've mentioned will keep the new supervisor alive for at least a year, with only a few bruises along the way. We've added a few more skills in this book that are important, and the individual jobs will vary enough to bring up the need for additional skills, but those we've mentioned are still the "bread and butter" skills for the majority of new supervisors.

# BOSS—SUBORDINATE RELATIONS

Let's not forget that in this chapter we're primarily concerned with the role of the supervisor in the organization. By our definition of supervision—getting work done through others—we create a boss—subordinate relationship. If we are considering being a supervisor, we must imagine this kind of relationship not as an occasional thing but as a way of life. Becoming a supervisor is in that sense a point of no return—unless we give up being a supervisor. As we'll see in the next chapter, we take on a new image, a new identity. We become the boss. If we are not comfortable with that relationship, then we had better avoid becoming a supervisor. We *must* think of ourselves as the boss. Like it or not, that's what our employees are going to think of us, no matter what we do. We can be lenient and try to be one of the gang, and the employees under us will say that the *boss* is lenient and tries to be part of the gang. We're still the boss in their minds. They'll only make the distinction of what kind of boss we are.

Any relationship between people is bound to be complex, especially if it is a continued relationship, day-after-day. Whether it be a husband–wife, parent–child, coach – player, or boss–subordinate relationship, there are many aspects and facets to it that can't be explained in a few words. Being the boss over a group of people, regardless of who they are, what their experiences are or our previous relationship with them, means that we're engaged in a complex relationship that we'll probably never completely understand. We will do well to think about these relationships *before* we become a supervisor so we'll be better prepared for the experience. We can study our own boss and the relationship we have; we can analyze why we like certain things and don't like others. We can study the relationships we have with people in other walks of life, outside of the job, such as little league or school organizations. If we have leadership roles there, how do they work out? Don't ask, "Am I a good chairperson?" but ask "What is the relationship I have with those people I'm trying to lead? Do they like it, do they accept it, or do they quarrel with me? Do they let me do all the work?" Finally, in this regard, the supervisor's role is to supervise all kinds of people, not just the good ones or the ones who like working for us. No two people under us will have the same relationship with us, and the more different kinds of people we have, the more complex our relationships are going to be to the group as a whole. The organization will expect us to be a good supervisor with *all* the people who work for us, not just select ones. We'll need to think about this before taking on the role of supervisor.

## THE SUPERVISOR AND HIGHER MANAGEMENT

We'll talk at length in the next chapter about our relationship with our subordinates—this new relationship where we are no longer a part of the gang—but we have to realize that when we take on the job of supervisor, *we too have a supervisor.* We cannot be free from supervision just because we are supervisors ourselves. We will have to be appraised, counseled, and perhaps even disciplined. We'll have to have our job explained to us; we'll have to be trained. We'll be taking delegation ourselves. In this new relationship, however, we'll be a part of the management team, and that brings about a different situation than we're used to as an hourly worker or nonsupervisor. When we talk to our supervisors we'll be talking about getting the job done to meet the organization's goals because *that's our job.* We will need to *think* as management thinks, as well as act as management acts. Our approach will be positive: How can we get this work done facing these obstacles (expecting to get it done), rather than thinking we can't do this because of these obstacles (*expecting that it won't get done*).

Our relationship with management isn't going to be limited to that between our boss and ourselves. We now have a relationship with *all* of higher management. One thing that is vastly different is that we will be expected to do our job without having to be motivated, without anybody worrying about meeting demands or going by a union contract (or set of work rules), or even using good motivational skills on us. Not that it isn't a good idea to use them on us, it's just that we'll be expected to perform even if they aren't used. One of the characteristics of this new job will be that management will take it for granted that we'll be doing our job, and anything short of that will be a surprise. If we are promoted to supervisor, it will be because of many things, as we'll see in detail later on, but the main criterion will be that somebody in authority believes without reservations that we can do our job.

The problem management has in selecting whom to promote is that the decision is more or less *permanent*. When we make a mistake in the hourly ranks, it's bad enough, but it is only one job among many just like it, and we can usually remedy it with a relatively easy decision—if we discover our mistake soon enough. Not so when an organization makes a mistake in the supervisory selection process. It's a major decision affecting many workers, and a much harder one to rectify. In addition, management is usually more likely to give the supervisor a longer chance to make good because of the many skills that have to be learned. All of this gives the move the degree of permanence we talked about. The counterbalance to that is management's expectation that we do our jobs and do them well. There's a lot at stake and they don't want to be bothered by our inability to get the job done.

To further complicate the situation, we won't be able to use the excuse to higher management that we're new to the job so we can't be blamed for our mistakes. We were chosen because they expected us to be able to handle the job, even though there is much to learn. When we go to staff meetings there will be some skepticism toward us. When we speak, it'll be taken as the words of new, inexperienced supervisors, and may not carry much weight. When directives are given, though, we'll be expected to take them, understand them and execute them, just as the experienced supervisors will do. If this sounds unfair, it isn't. It's the nature of the job we've taken as a new supervisor. There'll come a time when this won't be true of us, but it will only come when we've proven ourselves in the supervisory role.

## THE SUPERVISOR AND PEER SUPERVISORS

There is another relationship we should mention now that will be new for us. When we move to the new job of supervisor, we've moving into a new team. There will be other supervisors—some old, some new, some in-between—and they will form the particular team we're now "playing for." They have problems of their own, hang-ups, good and bad feelings about the job, the boss, and the organization. They aren't going to be our enemies, unless we make them so. We aren't competing with them, except in the normal competition for recognition down the line somewhere. There is every reason for us to get along with them, help them out, understand their situations, and expect the same from them. If we think of them as being our co-workers we'll understand them better. We should be prepared to give them the benefit of the doubt, not question their motives, look for the good things they do on their jobs, and so forth. As we think about it, that's certainly what we hope they'll do for us.

Many organizations are plagued with "in-fighting" among supervisors. Nobody wins in such situations, and of all the people who stand to lose from such a problem, we stand to lose the most if we are new on the job. We need to decide ahead of time that we aren't going to contribute to any "guerilla warfare" among supervisors, and we aren't going to fan the fires with rumors, gossip, or even truths that could go just as well untold. The safest approach to getting along with others is to assume that everybody wants congeniality as much as we do, and *never* suspect people's motives. We might question their judgment, but we need to leave the mind reading to somebody else. If we begin by being suspicious of everybody, it won't be long before we start seeing bad things in them we wouldn't normally have noticed. To make it worse, they will surely begin to treat us with the same suspicions. Then life takes on a pretty miserable viewpoint, and we start to dread the days we have to go to work. *It doesn't have to be that way*.


## CONCLUSION

Supervision—good supervision—has to be learned. There are many skills connected with being a successful supervisor, and sooner or later we will have to learn all of them if we want to grow to our potential. But to look at the entire list of skills and to think of the task ahead is a frightening experience. There is some hope, though. We don't need to have all these skills to survive when we first make supervisor. We have some time, if we can learn a few survival skills. These include delegating, appraising, training, disciplining, and communicating skills, as well as learning how to handle interpersonal conflict. With these skills learned to a moderate degree, we can usually survive until the others are learned. While we are learning these survival skills, we have to consider that we have the responsibility given to all supervisors and are expected to carry them out as though we were experienced and knowledgeable in all the skills. These responsibilities not only include getting the job done through others—which is our prime task as a supervisor—but also establishing a working relationship with our boss, all of top management we come in contact with, and last but not least, those peer supervisors we will be working with day-in and day-out.

## DISCUSSION QUESTIONS

1.  List reasons people desire to be supervisors.
2.  What is the one thing that makes the supervisor's job different from any other job in the organization?
3.  What is the biggest problem most people have when they come up through the ranks of the organization to the job of supervisor?
4.  Discuss the different levels of management and the function of each.
5.  Name the survival skills that are needed immediately when one becomes supervisor. What are other skills that must be cultivated in time?

## chapter two

# The Hazards of Being a Supervisor

When we begin to think we have a chance to be a supervisor we sometimes overlook some of the hazards the job entails. It is not the pot of gold at the end of the rainbow, nor is it the time when everything works out for us after years of struggling. This isn't to paint a gloomy picture; there are many rewards and nothing is as rewarding as being a successful supervisor. Nevertheless, aspirants to the job should recognize some of the pitfalls and be prepared for them. Only then can these pitfalls be overcome successfully. In this chapter we want to acquaint the people looking forward to becoming a supervisor to some of the roadblocks and hazards that lurk in the way of everyone who fulfills the dream of becoming a supervisor. By recognizing them, naming them and dealing directly with them, perhaps we can help overcome them as well.

## BOSSES AREN'T ALWAYS LIKED

If our goal in life is to be liked by everybody, then we're heading in the wrong direction if we're aspiring to be a supervisor. If our goal is to be respected for knowing our job and to make a valiant effort to deal with people as human beings, then being a supervisor will give us the best chance we'll ever have to reach that goal. The truth of the matter is that the very word "boss" has a bad connotation in our language. Rarely are good things said in general conversation about the boss. Jokes are made about the boss; threats are made. That's not very encouraging when we consider we're trying to become a boss. Going back to what we just said, though, there are rewards, such as self-satisfaction and self-fulfillment, and there is the chance that we will also be liked. It is not a guarantee that we'll be disliked just because we are the boss. It isn't a requirement of the job. It is possible for us to be a boss, and a good one, and still be liked by the people who work for us. In fact, we ought to think of this as *the rule rather than the exception*. At the same time, we should be ready to admit that there are sometimes circumstances outside of our control or based on previous events or former bosses that make people distrust us, or even dislike us—just because we are the boss, not because we are who we are. This is just one of the hazards of being a boss.

Why don't people like the boss? As we've suggested already, it may be due to something that happened before we came on the scene. It may be that the last person to hold the job had conflicts that were not resolved and were left over for us. It may be that we have to get people to do things that they don't want to do, don't like to do, or think somebody else ought to do. We may be perfectly within our rights to get them to do it. It may be an organizational decision or policy that we didn't have anything to do with, but are obligated to carry out. We may not even like the decision or policy. Nevertheless, in carrying out our job we may find that our action is not liked, hence *we* aren't liked. We can overcome it in time, of course, and we would be wrong to let it affect us so much that we neglect our everyday duties. We should find out why the situation exists as it does, but we may come up shorthanded. We may have to surmise how and why the situation got where it is. At this point we'd do better to just do our job the best we can, take advantage of opportunities to prove our good side, then let nature take its course.

# BEING THE BOSS IS OKAY

We must recognize that being the boss isn't something to be ashamed of. It's something to be proud of because we worked to get there, and we had some proven qualities that others didn't have. That's why we got the job in the first place. For this we should be glad, not sad! The organization is only as good as the people, and the supervisor is an important part of the work force. Somebody has to give the directions, follow up on actions, evaluate the results and take further action as required. All of this must be done within the framework of an organization's structure, and that's where the supervisors come in. Little if anything would get done if the supervisors weren't there to initiate the activities. Of all the levels we talked about in the first chapter, the first line of supervision—more than any other level—is on the firing line. Everybody above the first line can hand the work responsibility down to another supervisor. Not so at first level. Here supervision stops and work begins. Here there is interface with the hourly workers. Here is the real test of whether or not things are going to get done or not. In other words, *it's a job to be proud of.*

Perhaps it is safe to say that our failure and the failure of those around us to recognize the importance of our job is one of the hazards of the job of supervision. It can affect our confidence level if we aren't careful. It can cause us to get down on ourselves to the extent we begin to believe that bosses are really bad. It's a shame when that happens. There have been those who have quit striving to be a supervisor because of the supposedly bad reputation of bosses. Others have worked for it, then turned it down at the last minute because they didn't want people to think badly of them. We shouldn't let this happen to us. The only time we should really worry about this is when we've been the boss for quite some time, and then find that we've got a bad reputation. Even then there could be things that are beyond our control causing this to happen, but in this case at least we know that we got to be disliked on our own time, not on somebody else's time.

## PAY STRUCTURE MAY LOOK UNFAVORABLE

In many organizations the person becoming supervisor, coming up through the ranks, may find that the pay structure looks inequitable. People working under this supervisor may be making more money on occasions than the supervisor. When they add up their overtime—the supervisor is not receiving overtime pay—the supervisor's take-home pay is sometimes considerably less than that of the employee. This apparent injustice makes some supervisors wonder how it happened that they were the unlucky ones to be the supervisors while their employees are lucky enough to make all that money. A good question or not?

Actually, such inequities aren't as frequent as they are thought to be and often there are offsetting circumstances when it does occur. For one thing, the only way people will make that kind of money is to work for it. In other words, if the hourly workers are taking home a consistently higher paycheck, then they are putting in a lot of overtime, even with time and half, or double time. At some point they'll begin to ask, "Why do we have to work so much overtime?" Admittedly, the supervisors often put in unpaid-for overtime, and most come to expect that as a part of their job. Some put it in unnecessarily, though, and would do better to do a little more delegating. In the long run, the supervisor will make more money for the time put in, and has the opportunity for more rewards than the workers who work for the supervisor. The rewards may not always be tangible. They may be the chance to achieve a difficult goal; or the opportunity to see a person develop under the supervisor's careful direction; or the knowledge that the job was done on time through good direction and supervision. These are benefits that are impossible to put monetary values on, but remain significant. For most, this is satisfaction above the making of more money for more time put in beyond the working day. Finally, if the only real motivation for our wanting to make supervisor is the money, there are many who would say it's not worth it. If that's where we hope to get our satisfaction, the money-per-worry ratio may be too small for us. We'd better look for our satisfaction (from money) elsewhere.


## NO LONGER PART OF THE GANG

Another hazard we face has been mentioned already. When we become a supervisor, we have to give up the "old gang." If we've come up through the ranks and see ourselves ready for supervision, we should ask ourselves if we are willing to make that separation. It doesn't mean that we never speak to these people again. It just means that we can no longer have the same relationship with them. If we aren't supervising them, that makes some difference, but we can't hope that things will always be the same. For one reason, they will no longer see us as the same person because we are a supervisor, even if we aren't theirs. They just won't be able to be as much at ease as they were before, even if we haven't changed. Actually, *we have changed*. We no longer hold the same viewpoints we once held. Remember that a certain amount of the conversation we used to have with these friends was devoted to running the organization down, the boss down, the policies and procedures down, and so on. This may have been good-natured fun or it may have been serious, but we as supervisors will find ourselves in the position of having to agree with them and "betray" our management trust or we will have to defend the policies and be perceived as being "on the other side" by them.

If we happen to be supervising people who we've worked with before, then the problem will become even more acute. They may feel stifled in their conversation and may not be free to exercise their right of disagreement with organizational directives, actions, and so on. Also, we may find it hard to accurately appraise, as we'll see later, if we are too much a part of the gang. Definitely, we'll be in a difficult situation if serious discipline is required. It's going to be hard for us to try to deal with insubordination when we are going to lunch, taking breaks, and continuing a relationship that was going on during the time we were still a nonsupervisor.

Of course, it's possible to do this and not let it bother us. Perhaps we can keep up the relationship and do our job successfully. Some have done it, but many find it difficult or nearly impossible. If we decide to try it when we make supervisor, we should make a resolution with ourselves that we'll always be honest with others about our feelings toward the job and the organization. We don't want to get into the position where we leave them thinking that we believe the organization's policies are wrong, weak, or not fair, when we actually understand them and expect the employees to accept them. In the long run, this action will get us into more trouble than anything else we do!

## DIFFICULTIES: DISCIPLINE

It doesn't take much imagination to figure out that there may be those employees who will try to take advantage of our new appointment. Somebody is going to try to test us in some way sooner or later. This will be true even if we're supervising a group of people we've never seen before. They'll know we're new in the job of supervisor, and they'll be more likely to take advantage of us in this role than they would be an older, more experienced supervisor. We must be prepared to exercise discipline the best we know how, even if we do some things wrong. The rule of thumb we'll give is "never threaten anything we aren't willing to carry out, and never carry out any punishment we haven't explained ahead of time." The quicker we learn the skill of discipline and the easier it is for us to use, *the less often we'll have to use it!*

## DIFFICULTIES: APPRAISING

If we make the job of supervisor, it won't be long before we'll have to do some kind of formal appraisal of our people (if the organization has such a plan). But well before this formal appraisal, we ought to be getting a good idea of just what our employees can and can't do, just what their strengths and weaknesses are, and start some kind of program to help them improve. We don't want to wait until it's formal appraisal time to find out how good they are. But now that we've decided appraising is beneficial, we still need to know how to appraise those who work for us. What do we look for? How do we tell how good they really are? What do we use as a standard? There are answers to all of these questions, but as we think about becoming a supervisor we wonder how to acquire them. We'll be more specific later in the book and give some step-by-step procedures on how to do the appraisals. Two hazards that might arise are that we will not use a very good standard or that the appraisal will be based on something like opinion or prejudice, rather than on hard or tangible facts.

As we'll see in Chapter 6, we can only evaluate performance when we know what the standard for a particular job is, and when an employee also knows what the standard is. We can only justify our appraisal if the person not only knows the standard but has been trained to meet it. This must come well before the appraisal period, and should be established for the entire time the employee is doing the job for which we're appraising him or her. That puts a tremendous burden on the new supervisor to find out if there is a standard, if the employees know the standard, and if they've been trained to meet this standard. It's difficult and presents a real hazard to our success in the job.

# DIFFICULTIES: REWARDING EMPLOYEES

One of the keys to successful motivation of employees is the ability to properly reward behavior. Such rewarding is likely to cause the behavior to happen again; it reinforces it. Actions which go unrewarded aren't as likely to happen over and over. The idea of rewarding behavior may seem simple enough or so remote that it isn't even a problem. There are some things we can do before becoming a supervisor that will make the rewarding part of our job easier. We can look at the people around us and the job they're doing. We can ask ourselves what it is that should be rewarded, and what should be left unrewarded. We can look at ourselves and ask the same questions. How did we feel when we did a job well and nobody noticed it? How did we feel when we got some recognition for an assignment that we carried out from beginning to end? These observations will help us to deal with the matter of reward.

When we talk about reward as a motivation, we aren't necessarily talking about money and public acclaim. The reward may be no more than a pat on the back or a statement by the boss, "You handled that well." Of all the things that motivate people, recognition, responsibility, and a chance to achieve lead the list by far. Things like working conditions, benefits, and even money don't motivate us as much or for as long a time. Not that these things are unimportant; it's just that we may overlook the things that work the best and are the easiest to do, if we worry all the time about motivating people with money, better benefits, and better working conditions. It's one of the difficulties that supervisors run into: knowing just how and where to practice rewarding employees to get the most motivation.

## PRESSURES FROM ABOVE

Another hazard the supervisor runs into, especially one just coming into the job, is pressure from above. As a non-supervisor, we rarely think about the pressures that are put on our boss by the management at different levels. We also suggested that sometimes management crosses over the lines of duties and gets into another level's functions. When this happens, there are some real problems. For example, we've stressed that the supervisor has to learn delegation, not only learn it, but practice it. Let's see what happens if the supervisor is practicing delegation and something goes wrong. There is a mistake that can be traced to the fact that the supervisor had a subordinate doing the work, making the customer contact, dealing with the problem, or whatever it was. The boss at the next level gets a call from his or her counterpart one level up who wants to know what happened. As the mistake is passed up and down the line and the fact that it resulted from a case of delegation—perhaps properly so under the circumstances—levels begin to get confused. The top boss is upset because the problem got up that far. The word is passed down to see that it doesn't happen again, and when it gets to the bottom level of supervision, there is an edict, "From now on you check on those things yourself, instead of delegating them." What should be a first-line supervisory problem has gotten out of hand, gotten up the line too far, and people up the line are making decisions about things that shouldn't concern them. Not only that, there is now an order that prohibits doing the job as it should be done.

What do first-line supervisors do in a case like this? Do we just violate the order and go on with our business as usual? Do we give up and do it the way we've been told? Do we tell our boss the importance of delegation? Perhaps none of these is the right solution; perhaps a little of each is the best solution. We cannot put ourselves in the role of insubordination, nor can we decide that we're going to give our boss a management training program on delegation. What we can do, though, is try to justify our action and show the capabilities of the person to whom we delegated the work. Further, we can continue to delegate in other areas, building confidence in our people and letting our boss know that we can get the job done. While this may sound remote to one who is considering becoming a supervisor, it becomes a very real problem when it occurs to the supervisor. *And it will occur if we practice enough delegation.*

## JOINING THE FRATERNITY

One of the problems or hazards of becoming a supervisor is that when we do get the job, we'll forget what it's like now, not being a supervisor. We may join the fraternity of other supervisors, think like they think, look down on the hourly workers perhaps, become so organizationally oriented that we just plain forget how the people under us *really* think. We'll forget that they have feelings, that they don't look at things the way we look at them, and that they are real people like us. We lose a thing called *empathy*. Once we forget what it's like in jobs like ours, we can no longer effectively supervise our employees at this level.

How do we overcome this hazard? We can start right now by trying to make some indelible marks on our memory of what it's like being an hourly worker or a nonsupervisor. We can get a good picture of ourselves and others like us. What do we think about? How do we feel about things? Why do we feel the way we do? We don't have to justify our feelings or our thoughts at this time. All we have to do is to *remember them.* The broader we make this base, the better picture we're getting, so we ought to study as many people as possible. This will help us remember better and give us a clearer picture of the way nonsupervisors think. Just be sure that we don't depend entirely on ourselves for this information. The fact that we've made a conscious effort to remember the thoughts and feelings of this particular group that we'll be supervising someday will help us do it.

What about the idea that the people under us are to be looked down on? Does it really happen? We can see that the idea of doing it is wrong, but we might as well admit that there are those who look down on the hourly workers as somehow being inferior to supervisors. Like any kind of prejudice, such feelings stem from an effort to build ourselves up by pushing somebody else down. It's nothing new, and it will not end when we take over as the supervisor. (It won't even end if we take over as president or director of the organization!) The important thing for us is to avoid it in our own thinking. What brings on this kind of thinking? The usual thing is that poor supervisors, who don't know enough about supervising, end up with people who aren't motivated to do their jobs. These supervisors point out that their workers are *not* doing the job very well. It may happen because the workers are so united against the organization that they really don't produce. Even though their loyalties are misplaced, we shouldn't forget that they're intelligent human beings and this place where their loyalties are directed is offering them something that we aren't. It may be security, the feeling of belonging, recognition, or even a chance to retaliate for perceived injustices, but they have at least shown that they can have strong loyalties, and that they aren't void of the ability to feel and believe. We need to figure a way to capture this loyalty for the organization, instead of running the workers down. To a certain degree, it's the organization's fault that it can't offer enough appeal, security or recognition to claim these loyalties.

## CONCLUSION

There are certain hazards built into the supervisory job, and they can hurt the newly appointed supervisor more

"At least they can't say we didn't warn them!"

than the experienced one. There are things about the pay structure that look unfavorable sometimes, but these will take care of themselves with other rewards. There are difficulties in separating ourselves from the "old gang" especially as we have to appraise, reward, and discipline them. We'll find some pressures from higher management as we attempt to do this new job, but we can overcome these pressures if we understand where they're coming from and why. Our major task is to make sure we understand ourselves and others like us *before* we get the supervisory job, so we won't forget how to deal with people like us when we become supervisors. We can practice empathy (knowing what it's like to be in the other person's shoes) only if we remember having been there ourselves.

## DISCUSSION QUESTIONS

1. Discuss the different hazards involved in supervision, then suggest ways to overcome them.
2. List as many rewards as you can think of that come with the job of supervisor. Compare this with your list of difficulties.

## chapter three

# How Management Selects Supervisors

To the nonsupervisor, the supervisory selection process often seems very mysterious. Even to management it sometimes appears that way. But there are some good things happening in the selection process and it isn't a matter of guessing, tossing coins, or picking the person who happened to be riding the right elevator when the opening occurred in the organization. The most common process for selecting supervisors is by looking at employees' performance on the present job, and estimating how they will do on the new job. If we understand how the selection is done and what management looks for in the selection, we may improve our chances of being chosen when selection time comes around.

## SELECTION PROCESSES: PERFORMANCE ON THE JOB

It will help us to know how management selects people to fill vacancies in supervision. Our own organization probably uses the same method all the time, and we can find out fairly easily by asking our boss. If we think we may be getting a job somewhere else, it behooves us to be familiar with different selection processes so we'll understand what's being discussed when we hear it. As we've already said, the most common process of selection is reviewing a person on the present job and making a determination about the likelihood of success on another job, be it supervisory or otherwise.

When management looks at us to decide whether we're promotion material or not, what are they looking at? Is it just a matter of seeing if we work hard all the time? Is the amount of work we turn out the only factor? Is it just our "attitude" or is it all of these things? Is there some magic formula they go by that we can follow to be promoted into the secret ranks of supervision? Let's turn it around and see if the answer isn't a little clearer than it seems at first. Suppose we were looking for somebody to work for us, to get a job done for us that involved people. Further, suppose that all we have to go on is the person's present performance in a job quite different from the one we want to put them on. Who would be the one selected? What kind of people would we look for? What characteristics would please us the most, and what would we try to avoid?

With a little thought, we can come up with some wise answers to these questions—some accurate ones, too. Obviously, we'd be drawn to look at the person who was above average in as many things as possible. We might not pick this person, but we would certainly want to take a long hard look at anybody who had above average actions in certain areas, such as production, attendance, and knowledge of the job. These are obvious things, and we can be sure that they get attention from management. There are, however, some subtler things. We would want to examine somebody who was getting the job done with as little effort as possible. Some people just seem to make a major effort out of anything, and we'll have to admit that sometimes management is drawn to these people by the "smoke" that's stirred up. But we'd like to have somebody who got the job done with seemingly little or no effort. We'd take a second look at a person who wasn't all the time asking questions, needing assistance, speaking of possible disasters—but rather was getting the job done in a quiet sort of way.

Next, we'd probably be attracted to someone who was working well with the other employees. We'd especially be drawn to those the other employees came to for help and who were trusted by the other people. Since much of the job we hope to fill will include working with people, we're naturally impressed if the person isn't a source of constant trouble, turmoil, and discontent. We aren't as impressed, of course, if we find the person gets along by just giving in to whatever pressures are around, and tries to be liked by everybody. We'd look for somebody who isn't afraid to express an opinion, but can do it in a way that doesn't upset people. We'd like to think that even though some people didn't like the particular person we were looking at, they at least respected him or her to the extent that there was no doubt in the minds of the people around why we chose this person.

In our search for somebody to work for us, we'd hope to find a person who liked the job. Somebody who enjoyed the work, took it in stride, handled it day after day in the same way. We'd like somebody who didn't seem to mind that it was Monday and a new week of work had started. On the other hand, we'd worry about getting somebody who seemed to be waiting for a better day, better working conditions, or a better job. We all recognize that people naturally work better if they enjoy what they do and think it is fun. We don't mean that the employees should always be clowning around, cutting up, joking, or involved in horseplay. That kind of worker is often dangerous and frequently interferes with the work of others. We'd like a person who gets pleasure not only out of being at the job site, but out of the *job itself*.

This leads us to another thing we would look for, somebody who is loyal to the job to be done. We'd be impressed if we found people to look at who felt that their job was the most important, or one of the most important in the department or in the plant or in the whole organization. It would be fine—but not a requirement—if their loyalty extended to the entire organization and all its goals. If a person can get excited about one job within the organization, we should be able to expand that to a bigger operation. Ideally, we'd like to see people who had a sense of proprietorship about their jobs, had pride in the work, let others know it, and sought ways of improving the job and their job performance. Even when the job wasn't the most important, they could still see that it had to be done by somebody and since they were doing it they wanted it done correctly.

Another thing we'd look for is somebody who wasn't afraid of work, somebody who could tackle a job late in the afternoon with as much vigor as early in the morning. When confronted with a task, their first reaction is "let's get it done!" That would certainly impress us, and rightfully so. Such a person is a pleasure to have around, and would save us having to make excuses why we're starting it late in the day, or why it has to be done this week instead of next week. One thing that would bother us would be to have somebody who was always asking why something had to be done at all, in a certain way, or at a particular time. We'd naturally be more comfortable with somebody who had figured out that the quickest way to get a job done is to do it, not talk about it.

We'd like to find a person who wouldn't quibble about an assignment in terms of who is supposed to do it. Those people who check every assignment to make sure it's really theirs to do begin to grate on our nerves after awhile, and we'd probably try to avoid getting anyone like that for the job we're trying to fill. People who try to avoid work by seeing if it is another's responsibility end up avoiding work all right, but they also avoid work that really is supposed to be done by them. While they're finding out who is supposed to be doing it, they've already used enough time to have done it—even if somebody else was supposed to do it.

While we are looking for somebody to fill this mythical job we've created, we might as well find somebody who likes to take responsibility, or at least who isn't afraid of taking it. There are those who shy away from responsibility and they do it for several reasons. Some just find it is too much bother to be responsible for things, because others are always asking them what to do, how to do it, where to do it, or when to do it, and they don't like that. Others avoid responsibility because they are afraid of it. There's the chance that things won't go right, and that means they'll get the blame for it. They don't like taking the blame. They may spend much of their time trying to find others to blame for things that go wrong on the job they have now. They certainly aren't going ot go out and take another job that is likely to put even more blame on them. We can spot these people; they're the ones whose first reaction when something goes wrong is to find somebody to blame, not try to correct it, and then find the cause. We wouldn't be too impressed with somebody like that.

Let's see what else we would look for if we were going to try to fill this job vacancy. Remember, the job wasn't a supervisory one, but it did have as one of its characteristics, that of working with people. We're trying to show that there are certain qualities we look for in employees for *any* job that are similar, if not identical, to those that management seeks when selecting supervisors. Another thing we would

"I understand that the process of selecting supervisors is highly
scientific."

be impressed by is the ability to communicate well. We would like to find a person who knew what he or she was going to say *before* talking. We'd like somebody who could listen well and who reacted to what they heard, rather than somebody who was quiet, but failed to listen. We would hope to find somebody who only had to say something once in order to be understood, and who didn't waste a lot of words saying it. If we were really fortunate, we would find somebody who not only could talk well in a one-to-one situation, but could talk before a group if necessary. We wouldn't make it a requirement, but we probably wouldn't turn anybody down who could write well in addition to speaking well.

In summary, the people who would appeal to us the most would be those who approached the job with a degree of maturity. It wouldn't have to be an older person. Maturity doesn't necessarily come with age. What do we mean by "maturity"? If it isn't age, what is it? We mean somebody who can approach the job as an *adult*. Somebody who sees things in a proper perspective; the job is seen for what it is, no more no less. The importance of the job is understood, as well as the importance of the person in the job. The role of the boss is not over- or underrated. The person we're looking for can understand that people make mistakes because nobody's perfect. Because people make up organizations, they aren't perfect either. The adult approach is to give everybody the benefit of the doubt wherever possible—which is most of the time—so that feelings don't get into the decision-making process. The adult approach allows us to be accepted as we are, with both good and bad points. It also assumes that everybody wants to get the job done, since that's what we're being paid for.

What have we learned? We were trying to discover how management selects people by looking at their job performance. We made a hypothetical case where we were to select somebody to work for us in some job that, among other things, included working with people. We didn't make this a big part of the job and didn't pick many things that were connected with this part of the job. Yet, we ended up with a list of characteristics or skills that anyone—including management—would require of an employee when considering him or her for any job—including that of supervisor. We'll summarize the list a little later in this chapter, but for now let's notice that the characteristics we looked for would, in fact, make for a good supervisor. They weren't unrealistic. They were qualities and skills that people in all walks of life have, and they are things that any of us can develop if we put our minds to it. What we have done, then, is to develop a working list of characteristics, traits, skills —whatever we want to call them—for a person aspiring to be a supervisor.

When management uses a method of selection which involves looking at performance on the job, this is the way they do it. They look at people working on whatever job they're on and see how they are doing the things we've mentioned here. They find a very good parallel in our performance on the job, any job, and the predicted performance on a supervisory job. As we've seen, it isn't a matter of guessing. Nor is it all that complicated. We've seen that the things we would look for are tangible and measurable. If management has done a fair job of appraising us, they will have a good idea how we stack up in any one of the areas we looked at. Just as we would be able to tell, *so can they.*

## SELECTION PROCESSES: ACTING ASSIGNMENTS

So far, we've talked about selecting people by looking at their general performance on the job. We looked at the way they were doing their *present* job, and decided from that how they would do in a supervisory job. Management occasionally wants more proof of our abilities, so they go a step further. They give us *acting assignments*, where we'll be doing the things that supervisors actually do on the job. It will, in fact, be a supervisory job. Usually this is done when the supervisor is going to be away, either out of town, on leave, or vacation. There are at least two different approaches to doing this and we'll discuss them both.

First, there is the method where our supervisor is going to be gone, and puts us "in charge." This may mean that we have complete authority—the same as that of the permanent supervisor—or it may mean that we are limited to making only a few decisions. In either case much of the job is left to us, and we will be evaluated on how well we performed in the actual supervisory functions. We'll be evaluated on whatever came up, though we were not being "watched" on any particular thing. It's a good opportunity for us to develop and to show what we can do, as we'll see later, and we should take advantage of any such opportunity.

A second way this type of selection process works is for us to be given the acting job, but with an explanation that there are some things the supervisor wants to look at or we need to develop; we'll have an opportunity to practice and exercise some responsibility in these areas. It may be that we've never had to lead a meeting, write a report, conduct an employment interview, or set up a vacation schedule. We'll have the whole job of supervision (or as much as is given in the acting assignment), but these particular things will be looked at specifically. Here again, it's a great chance for us to see what we can do, and in a way it's a better opportunity than the first method. The accountability has been lessened on some items, and while we still have the responsibility, we aren't appraised on all the parts of the job. Obviously, if we expect to get a supervisory job, and get this far, we aren't going to blow it by letting *anything* get fouled up if we can help it. But we will know that we're being looked at and evaluated in some specific areas, and we can judge our own performance.

Acting assignments have many good qualities as a selection process. For one thing, it takes place in the real world. We are evaluated while doing supervisory jobs, rather than doing nonsupervisory ones. It's a fair process because we have nobody to blame if we make mistakes, and we get the credit if things go well. It also allows us to get a feel for what supervision is like. Who knows, we may even change our minds and decide that we don't want to be a supervisor after all! This occasionally happens. We'd rather find it out before we got the job than after the appointment has been made and we've given up our old job. It's difficult to go back to the job we've left, even if it's at our own instigation.

Whenever we get an opportunity to participate in an acting assignment, there are several things we can do to enhance our chances of success. First, we can show real interest and enthusiasm for the assignment. It is a great opportunity and we should be excited about it. Next, we should go into it with a determination of doing the best we can. This means that we will study the job with whatever time and information we have. Ask questions. Seek help. Read the reports and other documents that make up the day-to-day routine of the job. Be familiar with what the schedules are, how they are made up, and who gets copies of them. Don't be obnoxious about it, of course, but be sure to get as much information as possible before taking the assignment. Next, don't try to revolutionize the job in the few days we'll have to be in the assignment. We need to make our mark by excellence of performance by doing the things that need to be done, rather than by changing everything. Finally, don't panic. "Be confident and do our best" should be our motto. After all, if our best doesn't get the job done, we've still got a ways to go before being ready for the assignment!

# SELECTION PROCESSES: ASSESSMENT CENTERS

More and more, organizations are using a process called the assessment center to judge the potential of non-supervisory people. It is a carefully designed concept and is a generally accurate method of determining a person's chances of success in a supervisory job. We'll briefly describe it here.

First, the concept is to put people through activities that are typical of the things that supervisors do on the job all the time. These aren't haphazardly thrown together, but carefully and scientifically conceived and designed so that they will be valid in as many ways as possible. To further test them, the designs are used on experienced and successful supervisors to see how they handle the various activities. Anyone going through an assessment center will be measured against the performance of actual supervisors. They set the norm. The idea is that if we look, act, and react like typical, successful supervisors, we have a good chance of being like them on the job. Most programs of this kind have carried the validation even further by following up and observing supervisors selected under this process to see how well they do. The results look very good, especially when matched against supervisors who were promoted using other processes.

How do assessment centers work? A team of trained observers watch the employees being assessed, changing around so that each observer watches each employee at one time or another. This may go on for several days, and at the end of each day and at the end of the assessment period the results are compared by the observers and a profile is made of each employee involved. This profile shows strengths and weaknesses, not a pass and fail situation. The assessment center doesn't say whether a person will make a good supervisor or not. It tells how the employee rated against successful supervisors in a number of different skills, usually including things like interpersonal relations, communications, written skills, use of the language, decision making, problem solving, sensitivity, perception, organization, and others. This information is shared with the employee so that he or she will be able to know what the profile looks like and can take steps to improve as needed. It's a good system if handled by properly trained people, and the validity seems very good. Most of all, it's a *fair* system. That's important in *any* selection process.

## SELECTION PROCESSES: SPECIFIC TASKS

Occasionally, selection will be partially based on giving people specific assignments and seeing how they perform. This kind of selection process is valid in that it points out the specific task and usually sets a standard of desired behavior for the results. We may or may not know that we are being evaluated for our supervisory potential. The one problem with this process is that often it does not involve a people-related activity. Since we have no "acting" status, we can't be in charge of any people, though we can have responsibility for projects that may include direction of certain people. Also, we may have a job of presenting information to a group or conducting a meeting of some kind. We may act on the behalf of the boss on a team problem, or represent the supervisor at a project meeting or some other gathering. These are people-related in a way, and are occasions of great opportunity for us, if we take advantage of them.

What we've said before about making the most out of these opportunities goes for this process, too. We've got to be ready when a chance like this comes along. The moment we hear of it, we should say to ourselves, "Here's another chance to show what I can do, and another chance to find out what I can about what supervisors do." With the same excitement, we should immediately move in and get to work. We should find the goals desired from the project or activity, what form the results should be in, and how we should report it. If these things are to be left up to us, we need only to find out the limitations or restrictions we're to be working under, then get to the task at hand. The problem with asking so many questions in the beginning is that it may sound like we're frightened by the project and are looking for as much help as possible. Actually, in almost every case we'll be given all the information we need to complete the project, and may not have to ask any questions. This is even better, especially if we then take the assignment and run with it.

How do we work on such a project? The key to almost any assignment of this kind is *organization*. We need to organize our time, the work flow, the steps in doing the assignment, and to map out the checkpoints along the way. Rarely can there be too much organizing (unless we spend so much time organizing that we can't get to the project itself!), so this time will be well spent. How do we organize? We try to get an overview of the project in our minds by laying it out as nearly complete as we can. We may just put certain steps on 3 × 5 cards and arrange them on the table. Or we may get a large pad of paper and draw a flowchart of the operation as we see it. We may do it in block form or with a line diagram. In any case, we want to see as much of the complete picture as we can. Then we start making a list of things that need to be done, in the order they need to be accomplished. Beside each of these activities, we will want to put a deadline or completion date. It may be a target date, and we may have to start at the end and count backward to see just how much time is required to finish each phase. Next, we may want to add the names of the people who have various responsibilities, if we are working with others on the project or assignment. If so, we'll either want them in on the organization or send them copies of what we come up with.

Just organizing in the beginning isn't going to get the work done; however, it will help tremendously. It will assure continuity; it will give us job responsibilities and time frames. It will give us an overview of just how much is to be done and perhaps a little bit of how it's to be done. But it won't do the work for us, nor will it keep us on target. We will have to continue to revise it, check dates, and check with the other people involved in the activity. There may be stumbling blocks along the way, caused by people who miss deadlines, delays because of unforeseen obstacles, problems of poor planning on our part, or a host of other causes. That's why we made up the flowcharts or diagrams in the first place; we wanted to have some kind of guideline or checklist to keep us on target as we move along toward completion. We needn't panic. We just keep close watch on progress and make up the difference as we have to. Always keeping the final goal in mind, we revise the charts. Finally, we should issue progress reports along the way. Not a flood of them, but enough that our co-workers and our supervisor know of our progress. Remember, our boss gave us this job to see how we could handle it, and we're helping him along the way by giving progress reports. That not only helps us out in the long run, but keeps the boss happy, too.

# WHAT MANAGEMENT LOOKS FOR

In the beginning of this chapter we listed things that we would look for ourselves if we were trying to find somebody to do a job for us. Then we found that this list included what the management of any organization would use to fill a supervisory slot if it came open.

Let's go back and look at this list again to see if we can learn anything more from it. We won't list some of the most obvious things—those we mentioned but didn't discuss, such as attendance, production, knowledge of the job, general "attitude," and so on. The list we compiled looks like this:

Gets the job done with as little effort as possible
Works well with other employees
Appears to like the job
Is loyal to the job
Is not afraid of work
Doesn't quibble over who's to do the work
Likes to take responsibility
Communicates well
Approaches the job with maturity

As we look at it, we see that it isn't very long. Only a few items, but very important ones. If we were trying to fill a vacancy, most of us would be glad to have somebody who met many or most of these criteria. Now we have to ask ourselves, "If we were being considered, would we get the job on the basis of our showing on this list?" If so, then great! If not, then it's time for us to get to work changing things. Let's do it a little differently, now. Let's look at this same list, but this time give ourselves a rating score. We have four possible places to check. All we have to do is decide which statement is the most appropriate for each skill or characteristic. The ratings are as follows:

1. Not very typical of me
2. Could be me on rare occasions
3. Sounds a little like me
4. A good description of me most of the time

| Skill | 1 | 2 | 3 | 4 |
|-------|---|---|---|---|
| Gets the job done effortlessly | — | — | — | — |
| Works well with others | — | — | — | — |
| Appears to like the job | — | — | — | — |
| Is loyal to the job | — | — | — | — |
| Is not afraid of work | — | — | — | — |
| Doesn't quibble over who's to do the work | — | — | — | — |
| Likes to take responsibility | — | — | — | — |
| Communicates well | — | — | — | — |
| Approaches the job with maturity | — | — | — | — |

NOTE: If there is any question about the meaning of the above, go back and read the paragraph that discusses this earlier in the chapter.

Now, add up the scores by assigning one point for each check under the 1 column, two points for those under 2, and so on. There is not a norm for this survey, so scores won't mean much. However, a score of 27 would mean that our average is only 3, meaning that these things only *sound a little like me*. It would suggest that we need to have a much higher score than 27 in order to think of ourselves as ready for promotion right now. How much higher is open for debate, but if we got a score of 34 or 35, we probably didn't have a very good picture of ourselves, or we certainly are fantastic! What is more likely is that we got some 4's, but also got some 2's along the way, bringing our total down. If this is the case, then a 27 might be a good score. All we have to do now is to look at those areas where we're weak and start to work on them.

# THE COST OF BAD SELECTION

We've mentioned this before, but let's look at it again. When the organization makes a mistake and selects a person who becomes a poor supervisor, it pays for that mistake for a long time. It is a costly error. Not only is a job not being done as it should while affecting production, but people may be ruined or held back. The people under this supervisor are valuable to the organization, more valuable than the tools they are working with. If 5, 10, or more employees are developing a bad attitude or becoming bitter toward the organization because of one supervisor, it's sad and detrimental. It should not go on for long, yet it can and does go on for a long time in many cases. In fact, it can go on for a long time *unnoticed*. If higher management selects the person to fill the supervisory job, and the selection is made with confidence, they may not check on it too closely. Even if they do, bad morale develops slowly and is hard to spot on brief observations. By the time it is detected, it may take even longer to correct. Then there is always the problem of what to do with the person who was the supervisor. The selection may have seemed like a sound one; the person was probably performing quite satisfactorily on the job before the promotion. There's little chance that performance will resume if demoted. A change has to be made, but in almost every case, grief of some kind is going to result. There is no satisfactory solution. The bad selection created a problem that will be around for a long time to come. That's why it's so important for us to be ready when they select us. We must be determined that *we won't create that kind of problem.*

## CONCLUSION

Management selects supervisors in many different ways, but not in as mysterious a way as we might suspect. There are several ways that will give good, reliable data, and with a little thought, we can even come up with a good checklist ourselves. With some more effort we can give ourselves an accurate score on how well we would do if we were up for selection. Finally, we found that making a mistake in selection has a long and costly consequence. Management has to be very careful in their selection activities, recognizing that even with the best of procedures some mistakes will be made. We just want to be sure that the mistake isn't made on us!

## DISCUSSION QUESTIONS

1.  What is the most common process for selecting supervisors? List other selection processes.
2.  If you were looking for someone to work for you in a job that includes working with other people, what are some things you would consider?
3.  Do a self-analysis based on your list in question two.
4.  What kind of difficulties exist as a result of a bad selection in supervision?

## chapter four

# Understanding Human Behavior

Surprisingly, when we ask people what they know about human behavior, we are likely to get a blank stare. Most will end up by saying that people are' different so you can't tell anything for sure about them. Also, they'll say that since people aren't always the same, varying from one time to another, we can't even be sure about any one person all of the time. If we think about it, these conclusions would make trying to supervise people a very difficult task. How can we expect to supervise with any kind of pattern if people are different from each other and individuals keep changing? The truth is that people are alike in many ways and individuals don't change all that much. Specifically, it would be better to say that most people react in predictable ways to certain kinds of actions. If we expect to make it as a supervisor, we'll have to discover what kinds of reactions to expect from certain actions. If we do, then we can begin to predict behavior fairly accurately. In this chapter we'll take a look at some things we know for sure about people and their reactions to certain situations.

## BASIC NEEDS: PHYSICAL

Let's consider what the most important needs are for most of us. What is our greatest concern? This is a question we can't answer here, because it will differ for each of us and for any one of us at any given time. But wait! Isn't that what we said earlier, indicating that we do not know anything for certain about anybody? No, because look what happens if we put some conditions on it. Put any one of us in a burning building and what would be our major concern? Immediately, everybody has the same need: get themselves and their families out safely. Everybody is reacting exactly the same way to the same situation. We've found some common ground. This is a simple example, but it points out the fact that we can put people in certain situations and predict their behavior. If we can't predict their *exact* behavior, we can at least predict what problem they'll be trying to solve. We may not know the way a person will try to escape from the burning building, or if there will be panic or calmness, but we can predict that they will try to avoid the fire.

We can use this kind of approach to find out other things about people and their expected behavior. Suppose there is no fire, but we discover one of our children playing with matches in the closet among the rags and paper boxes. What is our concern? We are concerned for the safety of the family and house. In fact, we may rid the house of matches altogether. We may pass an edict out to the family that there will be no matches lit, no fires of any kind in the house. Now suppose that there is a blizzard and all the power goes off in the house, and there's no way to have lights or heat. There are candles and there is an old camp stove in the garage. The temperature is expected to get well below freezing at night. What do we do? We go back to the safety need and use the candles and light the relatively dangerous camp stove. When survival is at stake, we do things that we wouldn't ordinarily do. But if it isn't a matter of survival, we begin to worry about safety, because safety becomes our main concern. These are basic needs and we don't worry about anything else as long as we are concerned at this level. We probably didn't worry about whether or not we were graceful in jumping into the fire fighter's net to escape from the burning building. We didn't concern ourselves too much about whether or not there would be odors in the house as a result of leaving the camp stove burning all night. When survival and safety are no longer a problem, we'll start worrying about these things, but not before.

## BASIC NEEDS: SOCIAL

Once we get the basic needs out of the way and no longer worry about them, we begin to be concerned about other needs, usually social. We wonder about whether or not people are going to accept us for what we are. We worry about being liked by those around us, both at home and at work. These are our social needs coming out. They have to be met. Anything that fulfills them will probably motivate us. If we want to motivate an employee who doesn't have these social needs met, the best way is to offer something that helps to meet them. If we don't do it, somebody else will. Ideally, they should be fulfilled at home, but the home can never completely fulfill the social needs of people who find themselves working around others. Think about it for a moment. Suppose we were to come to work one day and find that when we got around our co-workers they suddenly hushed up and looked uncomfortable. Suppose they didn't include us in their invitations to go on break or go to lunch. How would we react? It's easy for us to say that it wouldn't bother us if that's the way they wanted to act, but that isn't realistic. We have to admit that it would concern us, and that whatever we did on those days would be less appealing to us if we were worried about why people weren't accepting us as they had in the past. If somebody came along and offered us a very challenging job, one that would give us a chance to develop our talents and gain valuable experience, we would be less excited about it than if we had these social problems taken care of.

What we're saying is that people need a feeling of belonging, of being accepted. That's one of the big things that organized labor has to offer to the workers; somebody cares about them, regardless of who they are or what kind of personality they have. In fact, the common expression we use in referring to membership in the union is that "we belong to the union." Imagine what would happen if somebody asked us if we "belonged to the company" or "belonged to this organization"! We would be quick to point out that we weren't "owned" by the people we worked for. While we don't want to be "owned," each of us would like to feel that the organization *does* care about us as individuals. We would like to think that the person we work for accepts us, as well as the people we work with. This gives us a feeling of belonging, and until we get that feeling somewhere, we're not likely to be motivated by much else.

## BASIC NEEDS: GROWTH AND STATUS

What happens when we get our physical and social needs met? Are we no longer motivated by anything? The truth is, most of the workers like ourselves already have these needs fulfilled. The average worker isn't worried all the time about the building burning down or being eaten up by wild animals or starving to death. For the most part, we have our "belonging" needs met at home and don't find that people are shunning us too much at work. People know we have faults, know that we do things wrong, fail to do things we should do on occasion, but they still like us for what we are. Unless we are just totally obnoxious, we are accepted among our co-workers. This is especially true if our bosses show us that they—and the organization—are glad to have us around and are willing to accept us as the people we are. Day-to-day, we come to work with those needs met, so the opportunity to fulfill them isn't much of a motivation for us. We're looking for something more. We're looking for an opportunity to grow, to meet some challenge and to take on some responsibility. These are the things that will most likely motivate us, if this is the case.

Suppose, though, that while we feel that way now, something happens that we lose the feeling of belonging; what happens to our motivation? What happens is that we suddenly lose interest in growing, in responsibility and challenge. We aren't motivated when somebody says to us, "We'd like for you to be in charge of this project." We would be motivated if somebody says to us, "We sure need you on the bowling team" or "We'd like for you to serve as employee representative for us in the upcoming talks with management.

In a way, it's just like suddenly finding out the building is on fire; we forget about our other needs until we take care of getting our safety or survival needs met. We tend to go back to the more basic need whenever it stops being met. By the same token, we tend to go on to the more advanced needs when the basic ones are met. For example, after we get the belonging need satisfied, we have another need that is present; it's the *need for recognition*. It's present in all of us and comes out as we get more of the basic needs fulfilled. Let's see how it works with a little incident that takes place in a carpool. First, let's introduce the characters and set the stage: Dave, Anne, and Bill have been riding together to work for several years. They all live on the same street, in about the same kind of house. Their job levels are about the same, though Dave has just been promoted to a level slightly above the other two. All work for the same company, though in different departments. Each has children in high school; Dave's son is a senior, while Anne has two children—twins—just starting their first year. Bill's oldest daughter is a second-year student, and his youngest son is not yet in high school. Dave and Anne do most of the talking each day, with Bill entering in either as a negotiator or to take sides with one or the other to help win an argument before they get to the parking lot. As we start to listen, Anne is talking about her twins.

Anne:   I just couldn't believe how fast they caught on to the routines. They had gone out for gymnastics only a month before both of them were being looked at for the high school team.

Dave:   That's great; I'll bet you're proud of them. They're lucky, too, because it's such a new sport not many people are going out for the team. They'll probably have a good chance to make it this year.

Anne:   (A little uptight) Well, I think they can make it because they're good.

Dave:   Oh, I didn't mean that they couldn't if it weren't such a new sport. I'm sure they're good all right. That's a tough sport. It's just that in a sport like football —where so many people go out for it—the competition is really rough. Even though he made first string in his second year, David still had to try out every year.

"It's okay dear — Daddy's just dreaming about his new supervisory job."

Anne:   Well, as big as he is, he ought to make it. I'll bet he'd have a rough time in gymnastics. (Laughs, lightly)

Dave:   Oh, I don't know. He's such a natural athlete, you know, things like that come easily for him. Like pole vaulting last year. He'd never tried before, but they needed somebody so he went out and made the team as their main pole vaulter. Came in first in one meet; second a couple of times.

Anne:   You know, boys are lucky that they have so many different sports to try out for. My girls will never know if they can pole vault or not.

Bill:   Hey, maybe they will! Suzie is convinced she could make the football team if she tried. If she gains much more weight, I may insist she try out next year!

Bill and Anne laugh at that, as they turn into the parking lot.

What we've heard from these people probably sounds typical of most carpools in the country. What has it got to do with a book on how to become a supervisor? It tells the story of the need for recognition. It's typical because here were two people discussing their children. (We say two, since Bill really didn't get into the conversation to talk about *his* daughter. Maybe we'll hear from them again, and see what Bill has to contribute to our education about supervisors and the people who work for them.) We tend to think that it's just natural that these people brag about their children, and that's just the point: *It is natural*. But why is it natural? What's natural about it? Why does everybody do it? If we say that people are just proud of their children, and that's the only reason, then we don't understand the importance of this little conversation. Just imagine that these three people had been on a fishing trip, and the conversation this morning dealt with their results on the trip. Can't we just guess what they would be saying! The first fish story would be wasted on the others, because the next person would have caught a bigger one, or better one, or would have taken longer to catch it. By the time the last story was told, the first one would have sounded like child's play. What's natural about this is that these people were striving for recognition, or as we've been saying it, they needed to get their recognition *need* met. They were doing it through their children.

Notice that Anne started off immediately pointing out how fast they (the twins) caught on to the routines. She didn't say, by the way, that they actually made the team, only that they were being *looked at* for the high school team. She was covering herself in case they didn't, while getting the recognition from the fact that they are (1) young to be considered, (2) out only for a month and being looked at, (3) learned the routines in only a month, and (4) had not been out for gymnastics before. That's a pretty good target to shoot at. How does one get recognition out of refuting that? Well, there are two ways of getting recognition for ourselves: First, by being better than anybody else, or second, by bringing them down below ourself. Dave chose the latter route. He decided to reduce Anne's status by pointing out that the reason that is happening is "because it's such a new sport not many people are going out for the team." Notice that he wasn't unkind about it, or so it would seem on the surface. He was excited, "That's great; I'll bet you're proud of them," he said with some obvious sincerity. Then immediately he went into the bit about not many people going out for the team.

Our need for recognition is not met just because we're good at something; it is met when we're better than somebody else at something. If Dave hadn't wanted recognition, he could have left it there, *matching* the story with one of his own. But he wasn't interested in *matching* the story; he wanted to have some status and one way to get it was to reduce Anne's status a little before telling his own story. It was a little bit of cover in case his football story didn't get as much recognition as he had hoped. He carried it too far for Anne, though, and she got a little uptight about it. "Well," she said, "I think they can make it because they're good." She saw through his attempt to reduce their athletic ability. He tried to cover his overstatement by clarifying. He said that he didn't mean they couldn't make it if it wasn't such a new sport, then turned around and said that's just exactly what he meant! Listen: "It's just that in a sport like football —where so many people go out for it—the competition is really rough." Didn't he mean to imply that they wouldn't have been looked at if the competition wasn't pretty light in gymnastics? Notice his not-too-subtle way of getting in the licks about his son David overcoming the competition. He (Dave) matched her story of being looked at early by getting in that David made first string in his second year of high school. That's pretty good, but it's made better by the fact that he has made it each year against strong competition that he has to compete with in try-outs, so there's nothing given to him. Score one for Dave.

But wait! Anne can't let that go by. She needs to erase the points someway by showing that David's feat isn't all that good. How does she do it? By saying that Dave's son is a lousy, no-good football player? By saying that football is a hoax and that you get in by knowing somebody? No, neither of these. She was much more clever than that, striking at a point where Dave could take no credit. She gave nature the credit, "Well, as big as he is, he ought to make it." That ended the recognition for the moment, and got her back even. But she couldn't leave it there! She sensed victory and moved in, "I'll bet he'd have a rough time in gymnastics." Now she's got him. David made the football team, not by skill, not against all that competition, but just because he was so big he couldn't help it. Now we can imagine that huge hulk of a boy trying to tiptoe down the beam.

Is Dave down and out? Oh, no. Not yet. He got off of football and went to another sport. Since nature was getting credit, he went all the way and pointed out that his son was a "natural athlete." That's one for Dave, too. From then on it was just a matter for Dave to clean up with all the good things that happened last year: never tried before; filled in a desperately needed position; made the team as number one pole vaulter; got some points by placing first once, second a couple of times.

How can Anne top that? In a way she admits defeat, except that she uses one of Dave's tricks. He implied her twins made the team—or might make it—because there were so *few* people going out for the sport. She reverses it and implies that boys are more likely to find something to excel in because they have so many sports to try out for. She wasn't willing to admit that her daughters couldn't pole vault, just that they would never get a chance to find out.

So it ends for this trip into town. They'll probably have another go at it tonight, and tomorrow morning, and so on for as long as they ride together. What about Bill? Why didn't he get into the act? He probably does when they're talking about other subjects, like music or hobbies or grades their kids are making. Actually, we found out why he didn't enter the "one-upsmanship" game. His daughter wasn't much of an athlete, and his son isn't in high school yet. It was interesting, though, that in a way he did get a lick in. He got a little bit of recognition by having the *least* athletic child in the carpool. His joke about his daughter playing football got the laughs, and for that he got a few points in the game they were playing.

## APPLICATION TO THE JOB

This has been interesting, but what does it have to do with somebody who wants to be a supervisor? Suppose we don't ride in a carpool? Will this help us any? What we've seen is a look at people trying to meet their ego or recognition needs. In this case we heard a discussion in a carpool. We could have followed them into the place where they worked and found the same things going on. The work place is filled with efforts to get some status or ego satisfaction. All this means is that we not only want to be accepted, but we want to be better than somebody else at something. We want to feel important, and the way we do that is to make somebody *think* we're important. We accomplish this in simple and complex ways, but it gets done at all levels by most everybody in the organization. At work, it may be a name on the door, our own desk, a different kind of uniform than anyone else. It may be that the safety people get to wear yellow hard hats, so everybody will recognize them. And that's what happens: They get recognition out of it. There is a certain amount of envy, some want to know why they can't have a yellow hat, and we know there is status because somebody wants what somebody else has.

Think what would happen in our place of work if somebody on the same level as we are, with the same seniority and the same job responsibilities, showed up one morning with a name badge with his or her name printed on it. We don't have a name badge. Badges are usually worn by management people. Our friend got one because of some special detail that was handled yesterday required it. It's no longer needed, but the co-worker liked the badge and got to keep it. How would we react? If somebody says, "Oh it wouldn't bother me," then that person isn't in touch with human nature very much. We would perhaps say we didn't care, but we'd find some way to either get the badge off that employee or get one for ourselves. Ironically, if everybody got one just like that one, it would no longer be a status symbol. In fact, if everybody were required to wear one except for one employee, not wearing one would become the status symbol.

How can we use this if we make supervisor? By recognizing that this is a need that most people have and that we can use it in our favor or have it work against us. If we don't pay attention to where the status symbols are, we are likely to overlook some important chances to build the morale, and may let something happen to hurt it. We may do no more than give somebody a desk by the window, not realizing that the window seat is a status symbol and that the recipient has less stature or less seniority than we have. The same would be true for a new tool, a new typewriter, or a new chair. As silly as it may sound, it has caused some real problems in some places of work when the supervisor failed to see what the workers thought was important. On the other hand, some successful supervisors have made good use of this as a motivation by giving recognition to deserving employees by using what the workers considered important.

There is an end to our need for status. It comes when we get it and are no longer worried about attaining it. Our concern is that we aren't growing as much as we ought to be allowed. We want a chance to do what we can, to meet challenges and to expand if we want to. We want to utilize our talents without thinking that the organization will hold us back. When we have gone as far as we can in a job, know it well, know that others recognize our skills, find little opportunity to grow, become bored doing it, it's then and only then that we're ready to be motivated by a challenge. When we're looking for ego satisfaction, challenge is a threat, because we might do something wrong and lose our status. However, when we are confident that we can do our job and feel secure in it, we aren't worried about the status, so we go for the satisfaction that comes from doing a job well. We are motivated by an opportunity to create, to use our imagination, to do something nobody else has done before. All of these things are exciting to us. So, when we become supervisor, we have to look at our employees and find out if they're ready for challenge or if they are still worried about status. Whatever we find out, we'll be in good shape, because we'll know what to do to motivate them!

## MOTIVATION FROM THE JOB

One of the first challenges we will likely get as new supervisors will be to figure out how to motivate the people working for us. We've been talking about filling people's needs as a way to motivate them. Let's think about another way to do this and solve the same needs. As we think about the different jobs we've had, including the one we have now, we can learn some things about how to get the motivation *from the job itself*. Think about the worst job we've ever had, for instance a job that was so bad we really hated to come to work. Now we need to ask ourselves, why was it we hated that job so much? (This is the key to understanding how to motivate people: our ability to analyze job situations like this.) What made it so unbearable? When we think about bad jobs, we begin to think of things such as heat, long hours, bad weather, boring, dirty, dusty, no chance to go anywhere in the organization, bad boss. In other words, we think first of the poor working conditions, perhaps low pay, the bad supervision and finally the lack of future.

Before we can learn anything from this list, though, we have to look at another one. Let's think of the *best* job we ever had, regardless of where it was, what we were doing, or how long we worked on it. What job—above all others —have we had where we couldn't wait to get to work, where we couldn't believe how fast the time went, and thought a lot about the job even when we were at home. A strange thing happens here. Note that as we think about this job, the list is *not* necessarily the opposite of the first list. We come up with things like challenge, responsibility, chance to work with other people, recognition, variety, meaningful job. What's strange about this list is that as we think about the jobs more carefully, we remember that many of these *good* jobs had characteristics of the bad ones. Often we had to work long hours, we had to work under miserable conditions, we got dirty or hot or tired or we didn't really make too much money. Why the difference in whether we call it a good job or a bad one?

The things that show up on the "good" list include some kinds of things that aren't on the "bad" list. Notice that the bad job list dealt mostly with things that *surround* the job, rather than the job (nature of the job) itself. In other words, the environment was bad. The conditions under which we were working weren't the best. Notice that the things that showed up on the good job list dealt with the nature of the job itself and our relationship to it. The key words are responsibility, challenge, recognition, and a meaningful job. Notice that these were missing from our list of bad jobs. From this we can find what is motivating about a job. It says that when there is some satisfaction, some meaning, some responsibility built into the job itself, then we don't worry so much about the conditions under which we work. When these things are missing, then we start to worry about the things that surround the job, such as how hard, how comfortable, or how long we have to work. There is some personal satisfaction if we've been given the job as "ours," no matter how small and insignificant it may be in the overall scheme of things. Just to be told "from now on, you're in charge of this," is a big boost for us. To hear the boss say, "If you want to know something about that you'll have to ask Charlie or Jane," is a real motivation for Charlie and Jane. The boss has given them recognition of the best kind. It has been pointed out to someone that these two people have responsibility and knowledge about the job that no one else has, and even the boss is deferring questions about the job to them. We must remember this when we get to the position in which we can use these things to motivate the people who will be working for us.

## DEALING WITH DISSATISFACTION

This sounds like supervising people is pretty simple. All we have to do is just give some satisfaction, some responsibility, and our problems are solved. Is it that simple? No, not by a long way. People are complex; we soon get into trouble if we try to reduce them to a two-step method of problem solving. People have been influenced by many things in their lives before they came to work with this organization. They will have had other bosses before we come along, and some of them will not have been as good as we're going to be! People have different personalities, different goals, and different things to which they react. We've seen that there are some things that most people have in common as to what they react to and how they react. But these are basic things. We probably could spend a lifetime and never know exactly what makes people act just as they do. Fortunately, we don't have to know this much about the people who'll be working for us in order to get the job done. But there will be some who will give us problems, and we'll have to deal with them.

Those people who are getting their satisfaction off the job, either from hobbies or other commitments in the community, may be harder to deal with. These people may be the ones who will complain the most about the bad job conditions. They might be the ones who will notice the heat first or be the first to complain about overtime. They might be unhappy with the wages before anybody else. This means that we really do have to worry about working conditions for everyone, not just for those who are getting their needs fulfilled off the job. We want to have the best working conditions possible for everybody, but we can be sure there will be some who will remind us when we fail in some way. For the dissatisfied we will have to understand a few things. First, there are some people who will never be happy on the job. This doesn't mean that they can't and won't perform satisfactorily. They may gripe and go ahead and do the job as well or better than anybody else. (We've already seen that there are some who smile, have a good attitude and are eager to work, but still end up not doing a very good job.) Next, we need to understand that we must try to meet employees' needs on the job by using the things we've been talking about. If we don't and we've done everything we can to make the job and its environment conducive, then we have to deal directly with the individual. We have to say, "Here's the job, this is what I expect, and here's the consequence if it is not done." It's not a threat; it is a statement of conditions. As we'll see in the chapter on discipline, the key to dealing with people who are likely to violate the rules is to set a standard, give the consequence for missing that standard, *then carry out the consequence*. This takes it out of the "threat" category.

## CAN EVERYONE BE MOTIVATED?

We worry a great deal about those persons who don't work very hard. As we think about supervising a group of people, we immediately picture in our minds some of them who are not working very hard. We know we can't solve our problems by firing everybody who doesn't meet our standard of conduct. We'd rather have people who are motivated without our having to do anything, but we know that this isn't always going to be the case. So we have to use some of the tools of motivation. Then we have to ask the question, "Can everybody be motivated to work well?" As we just saw, there are always going to be those who aren't happy. There are also going to be those who aren't motivated to work very hard. They'll do the minimum and no more. Sometimes less. We see people around us all the time who are like that. We get disgusted with them, perhaps occasionally we get unhappy with the organization for putting up with them while we have to work hard for our living.

There are some things that we can understand that will help us live with situations like this. To start with, we have to believe that in the long run those people will not be rewarded by the organization as much as we will. There are some inequities now, but they'll take care of themselves sooner or later. Some of that "taking care of" will be accomplished when we are promoted to supervisor and they aren't. Guess who will be the first to complain about our making it? Guess who will gripe because they didn't make it? That's right, and we shouldn't let that bother us at all.

The next thing we have to understand is that what these people are doing *makes sense to them*. Their behavior suits them in some way. Maybe they haven't thought much about it, but if you ask them about their approach, they'd have a good reason (in *their* mind) for the way they work and the way they talk and the way they think. No matter how irrational it may seem to us or how much we think it will hurt their chances for promotion, it will make sense to them. This is something we should try before we make supervisor: Pick out somebody who we don't think is working very hard, maybe even below standard, and ask this person for reasons for his or her performance. We can do this a lot easier now than after we've made supervisor. We shouldn't argue with the person. We shouldn't try to straighten him or her out, but we can ask as many questions as we want to. The person doesn't have to know it, but our goal is to store up as much information as possible for the time when we can use it as a supervisor.

# INTRODUCTION TO MANAGEMENT STYLE

What we get when we put all of this together is the beginnings of a style of management. A successful supervisor will have to find a style that is comfortable and one that works for him or her. What do we mean by a management style? It's simply our approach to handling the overall job. It includes the planning, organizing, directing, and controlling we mentioned earlier, but mostly it's the way we *habitually* approach the job. How do we react in a crisis? How do we deal with unsatisfactory performers? What do we do about delegation? What happens when there is a mistake that gets our boss into the act? How do we handle morale problems? What happens when there is a severe budget cut and everything has to be controlled more closely? How do we treat our boss when there is a problem with one of our employees that has got him or her in trouble with the higher boss? All of these things—and the ways we act —make up our management style.

Before we make supervisor, we have no style of management, of course. Since we don't have a supervisor's problems, we don't know how we'll act when we do have them. Since we don't have the authority to deal with the problems, we can't practice dealing with them. We'll have to develop a style of dealing with problems and dealing with people. Let's think about some of the approaches we might take. First, we could plan on not rocking the boat. We just play it cool, don't make any ripples, do enough supervising to get by, let the people do their jobs, and leave them alone. If the boss gets on us, we get on them. If the boss leaves us alone, we leave them alone. After all, they know their job, so why should we bother them? We'll delegate the whole thing to them and that way they'll grow on the job better than if we were bothering them . . . except that this really isn't supervising. If we don't get in and deal with problems before the boss is on us or before our people are demanding action, then we're *supervising by default*. Actually, we aren't supervising at all.

Another approach is that being supervisor gives us complete control over the people. They work for us, and that's what they ought to do: work. Because the organization has made us supervisor, we are obligated first to the organization. Our obligation is to get the work done. If it becomes a choice of getting the work out or being nice to the people who work for us, there's no choice at all . . . we have to get the work out or there's no need for us (or the people who're working for us) to even be on the payroll. This is the style of many supervisors, and we'd be wrong if we didn't point out that it is one sure way of getting the job done. There's no doubt that this approach results in a lot of production getting out and out on time. In a way, it's a "dramatic" way to supervise. We find ourselves giving orders, being in the middle of things with a steady flow of people coming to us for information and reporting data to us. This style works well as long as we're there all the time, or as long as the threat of our being there is present. The disadvantage of this style is that it puts most of the responsibility for the production squarely on our shoulders and very little on the employees under us. This means that if anything goes wrong, they simply ask us what to do, and make no effort to correct it themselves. Their chances for growing are slim, and since they aren't getting much responsibility or recognition, many of their needs probably aren't getting met. This means that we'll constantly have a motivation problem with them and that there is always the chance they'll go outside the organization for their satisfactions.

We could decide that if we can make these people happy by making their personal lives pleasant on the job without any pressures, they'll appreciate it enough to work hard all the time. The idea is to keep them happy, with the belief that happy workers are hard workers. We'll worry about their morale first, the job second. If we worry about their morale, they'll worry about the job. Will this approach work? Yes, in some cases. *But it has some tremendous hazards built into it.* When we begin to spend all our time worrying about the happiness of our workers, we have to put that ahead of the job. There will be many times during the day when we have to choose between getting the job done and keeping the workers happy. We're wrong if we think the workers will put the job first because we treat them so well. They, too, will begin to think only of their own happiness and well-being, and we will become more of a parent to them than a boss. We'll be expected to sympathize with their problems, both at home and at work. To complicate things, they will get so used to our thinking about their problems, worrying about their needs that they'll have a hard time understanding when we insist on meeting a production requirement, or when we discipline one of them. They'll ask each other, "What's got into the boss?" and wonder why we've suddenly turned on them.

Does this mean that we don't care about their problems? No, that's not it at all. We do care about their problems. We care about *them*, too. But we believe that the reason for their being there and for our being there is to work and produce. In other words, the people are there because the job is there, not the other way around. One other problem with their being treated in a way that will always meet their personal needs is that they never really take any sense of proprietorship in the job. They look to us for direction and protection. They like the relaxed atmosphere around the work place, but the environment becomes the important thing. They tell everybody what a great place they have to work, and what a great boss they have, meaning that they aren't under any pressure. If they need a few minutes off for shopping at lunchtime, they get it with no quarrel. They ask for the time off, expecting to get it, even making their plans ahead of time; they *tell us* they're going to be off for awhile, or they don't even tell us, knowing that "it's all right with the boss." Admittedly, they feel a loyalty to the boss, but not necessarily to the organization or to the job. They wouldn't want to do anything that would get us in trouble, and would worry if they thought we were being transferred, but not just because we were leaving. They would naturally wonder about our successor, whether they would have the same liberties. There must be a better management style than this approach.

There is a system of supervising that has some hazards, but also has some good payoffs if used correctly. One thing we can do is to build in responsibility for the job, giving this responsibility to the workers. We make it clear to them that we expect them to do the job, then treat them as though they will. When a choice between their personal needs and the job arises, *they* make the decision, not us. We simply turn it back to them and ask, "What do you suggest we do?" We make every effort to get them so committed to the job that they aren't that concerned with us and our presence. We are seen as necessary, but not a threat. It is our job to provide direction and training, to arbitrate decisions, and to solve management problems, but not to act as the driving force. We have the right to make decisions anytime we want to, and we do when there is something that we need to get involved in. We don't stand around and watch every action. We never give up being the boss, but we don't have to make ourselves heard all the time. We are concerned about the employees but we do them a favor by letting them have as much responsibility as they've shown they can take. We treat them as mature individuals, assuming they want to excel in the job, and we go on with this assumption until they prove us wrong.

When we give them this liberty to run the job, we are letting them get their motivation at the highest possible source —the job itself. However, when they do a good job, we don't stand around and pat them on the back like a proud parent. This implies that we're surprised. We shouldn't be if we've given them enough authority to go with their responsibility and then left them alone as much as possible. We set the perimeters, explain what kind of reporting we want done, and then wait for the results to come in. We don't lurk around and look over their shoulders making certain things will be done on time. As we will see in Chapter 6 we'll give them the *right to be wrong*, an important ingredient in successful delegation. Of course, we don't force this responsibility on them. We let them know when we think they're ready for it, offer it to them in small doses at first, and then increase it as they are able to take more and as they ask for more.

There are styles in between each of these, and a supervisor will go from one style to another from time to time. Frequently, we have to be totally concerned with getting the job done. When this happens, we have to have established with our subordinates that we're acting out of loyalty to the job, and know that they want to do the same thing. We don't make excuses. We treat them in the same mature way as always. We simply say there's a job that needs to be done and everyone will have to pitch in and help. Under this last style discussed more than under any of the others, they're likely to do just that.

## CONCLUSION

When we're considering the possibility of becoming a supervisor, one of the first things we must ask ourselves is what do we know about people. We've found that we know a surprising amount about people, and that we can even predict certain reactions to specific actions on our part. As we study the needs that people have, and realize that the things that motivate them are the things that fill these needs, then we can begin to understand how we can treat employees when we get to be the boss. Mostly, we find that when basic needs are met—food, clothing, shelter, and safety—people then fulfill social needs, being accepted by the group, or ego-type needs, recognition, responsibility, and a chance to grow. Successful supervision results when we're able to use this information and let the motivation come from the job itself, rather than from things that we do in our relations with the employees. Our relationship with them is important, of course, and our style of supervising determines how well these relations hold up. The ideal kind of supervision for most occasions is that which allows the employee to develop responsibility for the job as much as possible. We can be much more dramatic, however, in our supervision if the employees all look to us for all their direction, and if we assume all the responsibility for getting the work out. The easier way of doing it, though much less spectacular, is the reverse: letting the employees feel a sense of proprietary interest in the job. Only when employees see it as their job, will they get the most possible motivation from the job. And only then will the job get done time after time as it ought to be done. That's a worthy goal for all of us to shoot for when we get to where the action is!

# DISCUSSION QUESTIONS

1. Is it true that most people react in predictable ways to certain kinds of actions? What significance is this in relation to supervision?

2. What are our basic needs? How does ones motivation relate to these needs? Why is this information important?

3. What should be the source of the greater motivation? How can we accomplish this?

4. What is the key to dealing with people who are dissatisfied?

5. What is meant by management styles? Consider different styles.

## chapter five

# Things Employees Don't Like About Supervisors

One of the best ways to learn to be a supervisor is to think about all the supervisors we have had and figure out what we liked and didn't like about them. This isn't a foolproof system, of course, because there may have been some things that we didn't like that were necessary because of some of our own behavior. Nevertheless, as a general rule we can consider the things that employees don't like about supervisors as good indicators of things we want to avoid. In this chapter we will look at a list of things that employees mentioned most often when they were surveyed concerning what it was they did not like about their bosses. The items listed are not in any order or priority.

## FAVORITISM

Almost all employees dislike a boss who shows favoritism to one or more employees over the others. Even if the other employees are treated fairly or given what they deserve, they still resent it if an employee is given favorable treatment that does not appear to be deserved. While we sometimes see this in some of the discrimination problems that arise, it most often exhibits itself when there is no prejudice involved. This arises when the boss likes one employee better than the others, is a friend outside of the workplace, or an employee has a particular hobby or sports interest that ties him or her to the boss to such extent that favorable treatment is given. We have to be careful because we see ourselves less honestly than other people see us. We may not be aware that we are showing favoritism.

## WON'T LISTEN

There is nothing more frustrating than to have something to say to someone particularly about the job and discover that the person is not listening when we are talking to them. Employees say that they get very disgusted when they tell the boss something that is important to the employee only to have the boss ask later about that same thing, without having any apparent remembrance of what was said. Good supervisors are anxious to hear what employees think about the job and make every effort to get them to talk. There are supervisors who either don't think the employees have anything worthwhile to say or are so involved in their own thought processes that they simply don't listen to their subordinates. Employees soon get to the point at which they are no longer interested in telling the boss anything. Since the employees are the closest people in the organization to the actual work, it should be very important for us to listen to them when they are talking about the job.

Employees tell us that they get tired of bosses who make up their minds ahead of time as to what they want to hear, and pay no attention to anything that disagrees with that. For example, one employee might suggest that a certain procedure needs to be changed or that something that is planned to be done might not work. The boss just brushes that aside and says, "Oh, you won't have any problem with that I'm sure." At a later time when, in fact, the procedure doesn't work or a problem of some kind arises, the employee feels that the boss should have listened and gets disgusted with having to redo the project or spend extra time solving a problem that the employee had already identified. Perhaps an even worse thing to happen is for the boss to come in and see the problem and say something to the effect, "Why didn't you tell me that this might happen?" Now employees are really frustrated because they showed an interest and were ignored; then were accused of not being interested by not telling the boss about the possible problem.

## BAD NEWS

In olden days when a battle was lost a runner was sent back to tell the king or the emperor. It was acceptable behavior for the emperor or ruler to kill the bearer of the bad news. Employees tell us that this practice hasn't ceased today. Employees don't like bosses who punish them for bringing unpleasant news. It may be that an employee finds out that a shipment is going to be late. That employee tells the boss and the boss immediately begins to rant and rave, perhaps even cursing the employee as though it were that employee's fault. Employees don't like to stand and listen to abusive language simply because they were trying to help out the boss with pertinent information. What eventually happens, is that employees will cease bringing bad news to the boss hoping someone else will bring the news and receive the consequences instead of them. It is obvious that when we only hear the good news we're in trouble. In fact, since we have a choice of good or bad news, we should always choose the bad news because that usually needs some attention. If we get only the good news we think things are going along smoothly and consequently find ourselves in real trouble when the bad news begins to cause things to go wrong.

## USE OF RIDICULE OR SARCASM

One of the most common dislikes among employees is the use of ridicule by the boss. Sometimes bosses do not recognize just what they are doing or they think it's a good technique instead of just being open and frank. Many times the boss will say something to an employee like, "Well, you're on time this morning. To what do we owe this honor?" This is the boss' way of trying to point out that the employee is frequently late. The object is to somehow shame the person with ridicule without coming right out and dealing with the tardiness. Unfortunately, that's never proven to be a very successful procedure for dealing with a person who comes in late or otherwise performs poorly. A much better approach would simply be to deal with the person at the time they are tardy, pointing out what the standards are and pointing out how many times the person has been late over a given period of time. It seems a little inappropriate to punish somebody at a time when they are doing something right. That's the time we need to praise the person and not chastise him or her. Rarely is there ever a time when ridicule or sarcasm is necessary. Certainly not when dealing with employees. Ridiculing an employee in front of other people is a put-down and adults do not take very kindly to being put-down in front of their peers or anybody else. Ridicule also implies that the person doing the ridiculing is always right or always perfect and that the person who is being ridiculed is the one who is always in error. Sarcasm is generally used as a means pointing out inequities in a person's behavior. Here, again the sarcasm may do more harm than good, especially if it embarrasses someone. A sarcastic remark like, "I suppose it is asking too much for this report to be on time" will not build much loyalty or commitment to the report.

# TOUCHY OR OVER-SENSITIVE

There are some supervisors who wear their feelings on their sleeves and get touchy if someone even raises an eyebrow about some order or directive that has been given. They take it personally if an employee questions the necessity of doing something a certain way or has some doubts about whether what's being suggested is proper procedure. Employees tell us that they don't like to have to walk around on tiptoes, afraid to upset the boss, worrying because the boss is in one of his or her moods. There are enough handicaps in getting the job done without the boss adding to the problems by bringing feelings, personality problems or bad attitudes into the job also. While we recognize the boss is human and gets upset if the breakfast is burned or traffic is heavy, it's the sign of a good boss when these things are pushed aside when it's time to go to work and the job becomes the primary activity and attitude of the day. One has enough employees who are sensitive, moody, and have certain areas in their lives about which they are touchy without complicating this with the boss' feelings.

## NONDECISIVE

When we ask employees about what they don't like in their supervision, many of them say that they would rather get a decision they dislike than to not get any decision at all. They don't like it when they go to the boss with what they consider to be a legitimate proposal or request and the boss gives them an answer like, "Well, I'll have to think about that." What that usually means to many employees is that the boss either doesn't want to say no, so just delays the answer or the boss doesn't have enough gumption to face the decision. The fact that the employee has made a proposal or recommendation or even has a request that is important to them is reason enough for the boss to want to give an answer to that employee. Many times the boss will either be playing politics or may be frightened in making a decision on his or her own, so by delaying the decision, there's a chance the problem will go away and there won't need to be a decision. Some bosses end up never making decisions by either delaying the decision past the time of usefulness or by going to their boss for a decision. It's understandable that the supervisor is afraid to make a decision, and therefore will go to their boss because this removes any possible blame or responsibility for the outcome of the activity that follows. Such supervisors can survive for a long time in an organization but they aren't really much help to the organization and certainly aren't respected by their subordinates. Again we need to remember that anything that is important enough to an employee to come to the boss about is certainly worth enough consideration to give a decision. If we don't want to give a positive answer we need to explain why we are giving a negative one. If there is some danger in carrying out this action as a result of this decision, concerning such things as customer relations or money, the supervisor has a right to explain this to the subordinates in helping them to understand that this is their problem and that it could have some ramifications.

## OPINIONATED

Employees get tired of anybody that is so strongly opinionated that they won't listen to any kind of reasoning. But it is especially difficult for them to work in an environment where the boss is so biased that it really doesn't make any difference what kind of facts are presented. The boss' ideas are going to have to be accepted. If the employees get the idea that the boss is unyielding and unwilling to bend in any decision, they will soon begin to get the idea, just wait and let the boss tell them what to do or at best they won't make any suggestions or recommendations that are imaginative or creative. We never want to exclude our employees from the suggestion or recommendation phase of the business. As we've said before they are closest to the actual work itself and we need their help in finding ways of doing the job better or correcting some of the errors or procedures that exist in the present job. The boss is certainly responsible for the final action or the final product. Decisions about that action or product should be made on the best available facts wherever those facts may come from.

## MAKING UNINFORMED DECISIONS

Many times employees work very hard at keeping the boss from making decisions because they know that the boss tends to make decisions too quickly and there is never chance of changing his or her mind. As a result employees will sometimes delay asking for a decision until they have gathered a lot of information and worked up a very comprehensive recommendation. This way when the boss makes a decision it will at least be based on a large number of facts. While this sounds like a good idea, if the recommendation comes at the very last minute the boss won't have time to do the careful consideration that is needed for a good decision. We usually hear employees say it's when "the boss' mind is made up so there's no use in confusing him or her with additional facts." It's a shame if that happens. Because as we keep saying the more facts we have, and the more reliable the data we have to consider decisions, the better the decisions are going to be. That we aren't open to additional data after we have made our initial decisions would be a terrible charge to have made against us, especially if it is true.

## POOR TIME MANAGEMENT

Every survey or study that is made about employees concerns for their bosses includes a response from the employees to the effect that they not only are frustrated when their boss manages time poorly, but they are also disgusted because it affects their own time usage. When they go into their boss' office and the boss looks harried, is answering two or three telephone calls, is trying to make decisions about a half dozen pieces of paper on their desk, and makes it obvious that there isn't enough time to discuss any matter in any kind of detail employees mentally throw up their hands and say, "What's the use of bringing this up. There won't be enough time to do anything about it." Poor time usage is the result of many faults, not just something called time management. It's a matter of poor planning, poor organization, poor priority setting, and a general misunderstanding of the overall job activity. Nevertheless, when bosses don't manage their time well they invariably cut into their subordinates time. One way this happens is when the boss makes assignments at the last minute limiting the amount of time that the subordinates have to work on a problem or situation. Another way the boss cuts into the subordinates' time is by taking too long to check work that has already been completed, requiring revisions to be made in a short amount of time. Good time management is a skill, and like managing money it is something that has to be worked on all the time. You don't want to be like the boss who did such a bad job of managing time that all of the employees got together and gave the boss a good book on time management. Sometime later, they asked the boss if the book helped and were given the response, "Well I really don't know because I haven't had time to read the book"!

## FAILURE TO EXERT AUTHORITY

Employees want their bosses to act like bosses. They expect the boss to have authority and use that authority. They aren't looking for a dictator, but they are looking for someone that they can respect. Oftentimes employees develop distrust toward the boss because he or she has failed to deal with employee situations that are hindering the success of the whole operation. The situation may exist because an employee is not carrying a full load. It may be an employee who is consistently late. It may just be a malcontent problem. Employees as a whole generally want the boss to exercise authority and correct the situation. This is most noticeable when dealing with other departments or other peer levels. Employees don't like to see their bosses run over by other bosses in other departments or by other work groups. While it is not a case of getting into a fight and making a stand right or wrong, it is a case of exerting enough authority to see that the subordinates or the department as a whole gets the recognition, assistance, or decisions that are justly due. The subordinates don't like to work for someone who is mealymouthed, spineless, or in the vernacular of the day, a wimp. They want to be proud of, and to be able to respect their boss. They can't do this if the boss doesn't exert enough authority to allow them to accomplish their job. If they feel they are being run over by other departments or that others in the office or on the job somewhere are not being asked to conform to the policies or procedures they find themselves unable to give the respect due to this job. The same thing is true when employees have worked on a project and have decided a certain decision is the proper one. Perhaps the boss had agreed to the decision, then has someone else decide against the decision without the boss taking a stand. Standing up for people, right or wrong, is a matter of at least standing up for those things that appear to be right and giving the appearance of having the authority to deal with problems that arise. Employees naturally like to feel that they have someone leading them who is in fact a leader.

## THE DISAPPEARING ACT

There is a kind of ambivalence in all of us when we are working for someone. We don't want the boss looking over our shoulder and yet we want the boss there when we need him or her. Since no one is able to define when each of these times is, it's an impossible situation. Nevertheless employees get very distraught when they never can find their boss to ask questions, get information, or explain where to go with the next step in the project. There are some bosses who avoid decision making by avoiding the work altogether. They find excuses for meetings, take long business lunches, or visit other people in the office, in another building, or another part of the plant. They seem to have a sense of when there is going to be some pressure or some decisions that are not popular or a discussion that will not be pleasant; they simply disappear. This is frustrating for employees trying to get their jobs done, it is worse having a boss that disappears than not having a boss at all. Frequently these disappearing bosses don't leave anyone in charge, nor do they delegate any decision making authority. This is something that compounds problems. This is not to say that the boss should be on the job every moment of the day, before and after the worktime. It simply means that when the boss leaves someone should know how to find him or her. There should always be someone left in charge if the boss plans to be inaccessible. This is a good time to allow employees to grow, by delegating jobs to them, including the decision making or the problem solving. However, this needs to be done in a firm, formal way.

## LACK OF TRUST

Perhaps nothing is more discouraging to people than to not be trusted, especially by the boss. It is equally discouraging to not be able to trust the boss. This feeling of trust must work both ways. All of us like to be accepted for who we are, and especially when we have worked on a project or have obtained a certain amount of information and we go and tell the boss that we are going to do a certain thing. We like to feel like the boss trusts us to the extent that we have done our best and that our word is as good as gold. When the boss checks on us behind our backs or questions us as far as our integrity is concerned, we quickly get a feeling of despair. By the same token we like to believe that if the boss tells us that he or she is going to do something for us or that a policy or procedure is a certain way, we can accept that on face value. All employees like to think that when they share confidential information with the boss that it will be accepted as confidential and not used against us or other people. Trust comes on after it has been earned and when we make supervisor we start a sometimes tedious route to earning our employees trust. This trust is the most valuable thing and should never be taken lightly. If, for some reason, we find that we have violated that trust, or employees think we have, certainly an apology is in order. We not only have to earn this trust; we have to continue to work for it day after day.

## DISORGANIZED

Much of what we have said about poor time management and some of the other faults applies to this dislike. Organization is a skill, we get distressed when we see people who are supposed to be leading another group of people and discover that they just can't get their act together. They are disorganized in their whole life. The paperwork on their desk is disorganized, always in disarray. Their time scheduling is always poor. They not only are late; but they are also in a hurry. Anytime we see them they seem to be flustered or frustrated at having to do more things than they think they ought to do. Many times, the sad part about this is that while they are stirring up a lot of dust they aren't really accomplishing as much as others who may not appear to be as busy. Many times supervisors misinterpret their running around in circles, putting out fires as accomplishing a lot. You would hear them say things like, "I'm so busy I don't think I'll ever get caught up," or "I just wish things would slow down a little bit so I could do my job." The truth is that they could slow things down by doing a better job of time management. Disorganization has a way of affecting all the people within an organization, not just the boss. The work group gets their scheduling in the same kind of disarray. People are coming and going in all directions. The same people may be working on the same projects. Things that should have been done get left out. People get disgusted because they feel like they are spinning their wheels, waiting for the boss to get organized enough to tell them what to do. When they do go into a meeting with the boss there is no agenda, there has been no planning, and sometimes no notes are taken about what has to be accomplished. Important subjects get left until the end and sometimes get overlooked, together. A lot of time is spent on trivial matters and rarely is there backup or support data for the things being said. People tell us that it is very frustrating to organize their own time and work when they work for a very disorganized supervisor.

## LACK OF TACT

Some supervisors just don't understand that people have feelings and sometimes don't like to be addressed in a blunt manner. Employees often tell us that they realize the boss doesn't mean anything by what he said, but that they do wish it was said in a pleasant manner. Some supervisors get so caught up in the job and the urgency of the job that they just end up telling people to do things or criticizing people and sometimes hurting their feelings without even knowing it. Tact is an important part of good supervision and those supervisors who have learned it recognize that it's worth the few extra minutes to soothe somebody's feelings, let them down easily, or give a little bit of recognition or praise when criticism is also necessary.

## THE AUTOCRAT

Some supervisors interpret being the boss as meaning that they need to take an iron hand or use an iron fist to accomplish things. Their idea is that the boss gives orders and the subordinates execute these orders, and there should be no question about either role. Sometimes people change when they become supervisors, simply because they have had an autocratic, dictatorial, or dominating supervisor in the past and feel that's what the organization expects of them too. That's really too bad because there are a lot of ways to get the job done without demanding that it gets done, or without being totally autocratic. One of the best things supervisors can do is get the employees to contribute information or ideas about how to improve the job. We've mentioned that a number of times and will continue to do so. The one thing we know for certain is that when we have an autocrat for a supervisor we're not going to get many suggestions from the employees. The employees tend to steer clear of the boss and they avoid unnecessary conversation. If they have a suggestion they make it to one of the other employees during lunchtime, or in the carpool on the way home, but rarely to the boss. This means that the boss is totally without assistance in getting improvements done on the job. Whatever improvements are made have to come from the boss or someone else outside the department. This is a waste of good talent, and in no way builds commitment to the job on the part of the employees. Employees tell us that it is very difficult to go to work when they work for someone who is totally autocratic, unyielding in any way, and views the job of supervisor as one of constantly giving orders and checking to see that the orders are carried out. The autocrat seldom gives employees the chance to participate in the decision making; consequently, all that good talent is lost.

# CRUDE OR VULGAR LANGUAGE

Almost every survey of employees gives information that suggests that many employees are not at all impressed by supervisors who are very crude and vulgar in their conversations, either with them or other people. We hear comments like, "I wish the boss would study the dictionary sometimes so his or her vocabulary would improve." Not necessarily a moral issue, it's just that sometimes it is embarrassing having a boss who has what we call a "bowel mouth." Perhaps an even worse situation is that some supervisors only use this when they are chastizing an employee for some reason. It becomes much more pointed when it is used in this manner and certainly much more repulsive. You have to remember that virtually no one is ever offended when we don't use crude, vulgar language. Even if there is only one employee who is offended in some way, either he or she resents it or feels uncomfortable with it, we gain nothing by using it.

## VARIABLE PERSONALITY

We have already talked about the person who is inconsistent and the person who seems to be oversensitive, but perhaps the most frustrating of the personalities is the kind that is never stable. Employees could get frustrated over the boss that is sometimes happy, sometimes sad, sometimes in a good mood, sometimes in a bad mood, sometimes depressed, sometimes very touchy, sometimes very humorous, and perhaps most frustrating of all is the boss that is unpredictable in personality changes. Almost on the spur of the moment the boss may change from being one type of person to another type. This is certainly a miserable environment to work in because employees have to spend so much time trying to predict how the boss is going to react to whatever they do that they can't get the job done. We have already pointed out the fact that bosses get burned toast and get caught in traffic jams, but we've seen that there is no excuse for taking it out on the employees. While nobody has the ability to keep an absolutely even personality at all times, day or night, good supervisors find ways of evening out their personalities so that they are reasonably predictable. Certainly the employees have a right to expect them to do their job to know what to expect from the boss. In fact employees tell us that they would rather have a mean boss than one who is totally unpredictable. There are things we can do to watch ourselves and to ensure that we don't fall into the trap of changing our personalities. Perhaps the easiest thing to do is to make sure we don't get caught up in "highs" and "lows" as it is sometimes expressed. Even being too excited, too generous, or too pleasant can become a hardship because we can't hold that level all the time. It might be better for us to maintain a reasonably sober personality with a spark of humor on occasions. We don't have to be funny to be liked. Not everybody that is funny is liked, but people who are consistently cross would do well to change their personality to being a little more pleasant all of the time.

# POOR PLANNER

We've talked about managing time and being organized. In the heart of both, time management and organization provides a basis for good planning; but we need to say a few things about people who don't plan anything before they do it. We're not talking about the person who occasionally forgets something or occasionally overlooks an item in a meeting. Employees tell us that they really hate to work for a boss who makes no effort to plan anything in advance. We can get a mental picture of the poor planner as one who comes in in the morning, hears the telephone ringing, gets a request for something out of the files and in the next scene disappears over to the file drawer, overcoat and hat still on, with the telephone cord going in with the boss. When employees are called in for a meeting or conference or even counseling session they like for the boss to have planned it ahead of time. They get terribly uneasy with haphazard approaches to things that could be scheduled easily in advance or things that would go much faster if they were better planned. They are embarrassed when their boss conducts a meeting without an agenda, stated objectives, or desired outcome. They don't enjoy working for a boss who makes a telephone call on the spur of the moment and then makes up items that need to be discussed during the conversation. You can see the eyes turn towards the ceiling in a look of disgust when these bosses come in from a meeting across town, in another part of the plant, or even in the office next door only to say that they forgot to ask them about thus and thus. Employees are never very surprised at this because they know the boss is not a good planner. Informal studies tell us that a few minutes of planning each day will enable us to have a great deal more time available to us during the day.

## POOR COMMUNICATOR

Imagine the effect on employees when the boss comes in, gives a set of instructions, leaves and the employees look at each other and say, "Now what is it we're supposed to do?" None of us like poor communication, but least of all we do not like to work for somebody who is difficult to understand. We don't like being around people who tell us three or four times what it is they want to do, and each time it sounds like a different set of instructions. The process of communicating is not that complicated. The main thing is we have to know what it is we want to communicate before we start communicating. When we call someone in the office, make a telephone call, or go to see someone, we should know what it is we want to say, what the points are, and how we want to present the information. Good supervisors frequently write these things down even when they are making a telephone call. Second, a good communicator knows when the message was understood. This is usually done by some form of feedback, where the person being communicated to either repeats what has just been said, is allowed to express opinions, or describes certain actions to be taken as a result of what has been said. This way the communicator knows that the message was delivered accurately. There is another aspect of good communicating which is the hardest skill to learn, the easiest skill to forget and the one least often done. This is the skill of listening.

We never have developed very good talents for listening. Many times we are more anxious to talk ourselves than to listen to the other person talk, even when the other person is talking, we find ourselves merely waiting until they finish and then go on with what we intended to say without letting what they say influence us.

## DISHONESTY

We talked about trust and the fact that employees like to be believed when they say something and that they like to believe the boss when the boss says something. Dishonesty is deeper than that. Dishonesty is an intent to defraud somebody of something or to accomplish something by dishonest methods. It's very difficult to believe someone when you see them constantly being dishonest with other people. When the boss tells a secretary to say that he or she is out of the office because he doesn't want to talk to somebody, it sets a pattern for the secretary who may doubt what the boss says in other areas. Some bosses are so dishonest that they expect employees to lie for them by actually making statements or signing pieces of paper or somehow indicating that a job has been done, which has not been done or that work was done in a certain way. Employees don't like to have to cover up for the boss by misrepresenting the truth. As supervisors, we need to recognize the importance of not only being honest but making it easy for our employees to be honest. If there were no other reason in the world to be honest a good reason to tell the truth is so we don't have to remember what we said! When we lie we usually have to tell another lie to cover up for that one. When we tell the truth the truth stands alone.

There are no doubts that there are many other things employees don't like, but this is a comprehensive list given to us by a large number of employees who were surveyed and simply asked the question, "Tell us things that you don't like about bosses." When we become supervisors this will be a good chapter to go to. When we're able to overcome the things that are listed here there'll be no doubt that we will be *super* supervisors.

## DISCUSSION QUESTIONS

1.  Make a list of the characteristics that describe the best boss you've ever had. Prioritize that list, with the most important first, and so on. Compare your list with those of others and see if there is any common ground.

2.  Some say that we believe bosses are bad only because we each place different expectations on bosses. Since we're all different and have different needs, there is no way the boss can ever satisfy everyone. Discuss this idea and come to a conclusion based on the discussions in this chapter.

3.  If we've all had bad bosses, and most anyone can tell us what they like or don't like in a boss, discuss why it is that some people do not make good supervisors.

4.  Make a list of the characteristics that describe the worst boss you've ever had and prioritize that list. Decide which of these we are most likely to have because we've never been a supervisor.

5.  Pick five of the things listed in this chapter that employees don't like about bosses. Try to determine how and why bosses act in this manner. See if there

are things that tend to make it natural for a person to fall into the trap of having these characteristics.

6. Imagine that you are a boss and your employees are listing the things you do that they don't like. Decide whether you would be able to predict what would be on their list. Do the same for their listing of your good characteristics.

## chapter six

# Supervisory Skills: Appraising

Each of us has probably been through one or more appraisals of some kind. We've sat down with our boss, perhaps, and discussed our progress. The boss has told us how we are doing, where we could improve and maybe even set up a plan for that improvement. Sometime during that session we looked at all the things we were supposed to be doing, and the result was that we knew how the boss felt about our strengths and weaknesses. There may have been an abundance of paperwork, only a few notes, or none at all. We may or may not have had to sign a document that went into our personnel file. We may have had a chance to agree or disagree. Altogether, in whatever set of circumstances, what we were having was an appraisal. Before we are made supervisors, we don't think much about the role the boss plays in this exercise. Our concerns are mostly about how we are seen by the boss, and what will go on our records. As we view the possibility of becoming a supervisor ourselves, we begin to realize that appraisals are a way of life for anyone who supervises a group of people. Not only will we continue to be scrutinized by our boss, but we'll have the task of continuously evaluating the performance of the people working for us. It's not an easy job, nor one to be taken lightly. The success of *our* job may depend on how well we are able to appraise our employees and help them improve and work to their full capacity. There are some specific steps to doing proper appraising, and we'll look at those in this chapter.

## WHY APPRAISE?

We've said that appraisals are a way of life for the supervisor, but we've also seen that few of us really have thought about them from the supervisor's point of view. Mostly we have thought about them from our own viewpoint, and that should be a clue for us as supervisors. While we grow to expect appraisals, our employees may wonder why we have them at all. There are several reasons, all of them justifiable. First, and foremost, every employee deserves to know how we feel about his or her work. An employee's performance is a personal thing and whole careers are determined by performance day-to-day. As that performance is recorded as a part of a permanent file, it will usually be there for a long time for many people to see. It will be hard to change the words written there, even when the performance is changed. Let's see how that happens in this exchange between a supervisor, Jan, and one of her subordinates, Carol. Jan has moved over from another job to head up the group where Carol has been working for several years. They didn't know each other before this, and Jan has had the supervisory job over this group for about six months. They have been involved in a discussion about Carol's work for several minutes when we begin to listen in. For the most part, Jan has just been going over the specific duties of Carol, as Jan sees them, and hasn't discussed performance yet. Carol has said very little at this point.

Jan: So, as far as I can see, we're pretty much in agreement about what it is you're supposed to be doing. Is that right?

Carol: Yeah, I guess so. Sounds okay to me.

Jan: Well, if you have any disagreement, now's the time to say so. There are a few things I'd like to point out about your work, and we ought to be sure we're talking about the same job when I do. Any questions?

Carol: Uh, no, I think you've got it pretty well lined up.

Jan: Fine, then. By the way, before I go any further, let point out that I've been pretty well pleased with your progress since I've been in this group. When I took over the job, I purposefully went through every personnel folder of each employee so I'd know you better.

Carol: Oh, you did. I didn't know that.

Jan: Yes, I sure did. And I don't mind telling you that some of the things in there weren't the best. That's why I've been proud of you. As you no doubt know, you weren't rated too high on your last appraisal about a year ago. I noticed you signed it just as it was. It said you had some attitude problems . . .

Carol: Wait a minute! I don't remember that!

Jan: Well, maybe that's just my interpretation. It said you weren't too interested in your job, as I remember it. I can look it up if . . .

Carol: No, that's all right. I just didn't know that stuff like stayed on the records.

Let's stop here and point out several things. We're asking the question why appraise; we're pointing out reasons why we have to be careful with what we say because it's going to be on the record for a long time. More importantly, we're showing how careers, opinions of supervisors, and even attitudes can be affected by what we put there. When Jan took over this group, she read all the files. In Carol's file she saw that Carole wasn't interested in the job she had at that time. She went a step further; she added her own interpretation to that. Rather than considering that Carol had a bad or boring job, she decided it was an *attitude* problem. From that time on, Jan has been looking at Carol as someone with a bad attitude. No doubt anything that Carol did that *looked* as if it might have resulted from a bad attitude, Jan attributed it to that. Notice that her evaluation was that she was "pleased with your progress." Suppose Jan hadn't seen anything about Carol's performance when she took over as supervisor. What would she have said about Carol's performance since taking over? What does she say about the others in the group who didn't have these things written on their records? The point is, Carol had to overcome a supposedly bad record, the others didn't. To that extent, she's been working under a handicap, just because of something written on the record. No doubt, her career will be influenced a little by Jan's misinterpretation.

Another reason for appraisals is to give the people being appraised some direction as to their personal growth. As they are told their strengths and weaknesses, they are also told what direction to take so that they might do their best in the organization. If we feel they have a lot of potential in the writing end of the business, we might encourage them to pursue those jobs that include a great deal of writing. If they have shown talent for public speaking, selling, or organizing, we will want to tell them where such talent can be used in the organization. This doesn't mean that they should only head in the direction where they presently have talent; we hope they will continue to develop other talents, but good supervisors will always want to utilize already-developed talent to its maximum.

While they are looking at those already existing talents, we can also show them how to grow in areas where they presently have weaknesses. We should always be careful not to push people into areas where they have little or no talent. We've all seen supervisors who were never satisfied until they had tried to get everybody to do everything, even when some of the people really didn't have talents in some areas of work. To make it worse, the supervisors then gave the employees a poor rating because the employees weren't doing the job well. This is a trap for the employees. If they don't try to do the work they aren't skilled in, they get marked down by their supervisor, and if they do try it and do poorly, they still get marked down.

While the appraisal shouldn't be thought of as a disciplinary procedure, we can use it as a means to improve job performance. When the employees aren't performing as they should and we have an opportunity to point it out in specific ways in an appraisal session, we can certainly expect the job to improve. In fact, as we'll discuss in detail later, plans ought to be made at the time of the interview to review any unsatisfactory work within a few weeks to see if there is improvement. Perhaps the worst trap we can fall into is to think of an appraisal as something that is separate and apart from the job, and that happens once a year and is put aside until the next year rolls around. There is no follow-up, no review, no effort made to let the employee improve (with guidance from us) and no mention made of it —unless we need some kind of documentation for disciplinary purposes.

A final reason for appraising people is so that they will know how we see the job they should be doing. Jobs change from time to time, and occasionally we fail to communicate these changes to the employees. For a fair appraisal it is necessary to ensure that we and the people being appraised know what the job is and what its standard is. There should not be appraisals in areas where the employees didn't know they were supposed to be doing a job or where they didr.'t know what the standard for that job was. If they don't know it, they should be told immediately and not at appraisal time.


## WHAT DO WE APPRAISE?

All this brings us to the obvious question of what it is that we look for in an appraisal? In our present job what would we want the boss to look for? We probably wouldn't be too excited if he or she gave us a temporary assignment a week or two before the appraisal and then based most of'the job rating on how well we did that task. In fact, we'd like to think that the boss is going to look at our performance over the entire appraisal period and not just a few days or weeks. Evidence shows that many supervisors are highly influenced by performance during the last few days of an appraisal period. Knowing they will write a formal appraisal for each employee, supervisors may look more closely at a person than when they are not thinking about appraisals. This means that the appraisal isn't a true picture of the person's performance for the period, but only a look at a small portion of it. Of course, if we've done a bad job for most of the period and want a good appraisal (and know when it's going to be), then we can shape up near the end and still come out all right.

Thinking some more about what we would want the boss to look at, we find that we would prefer not to be appraised

"Yes, he mows the lawn on Saturday morning — uh — I'd rate it about 7.5 on a 10 point scale."

on those things for which we had received no training. There are times when we are asked to do something and it's not convenient to train us right away, so we go ahead and do the job the best we can until the training comes along. We ask somebody else who's now doing the job how to do it, or we watch somebody perform, or we may just dive in and start doing it. We practice a trial-and-error approach, sometimes doing it right, sometimes wrong. It's unfair of the supervisor to bring this part of the job into the appraisal as though it were a regular part of our job, and as though we'd been trained for it. We'd much rather be appraised on the things for which we were properly trained, had been corrected on, reviewed on, and given the okay as being able to do that particular skill according to standard.

When we're appraised, we prefer to be evaluated on the things we do that are *measurable*, and not those things that are merely feelings the boss has. This was what was happening with Jan and Carol. It was on Carol's record that she wasn't interested in the job. That's a hard thing to measure. It would have been better to have listed the details of her performance that made the supervisor *think* Carol wasn't interested. There was some kind of behavior or action that made the boss put this in the record. But the record didn't reveal that. It revealed an *opinion* that was the result of the behavior. If Carol were coming in late, not finishing a job once it was started, leaving late, or taking too long a break, these actions should have been on the appraisal. These are behaviors, and they can be corrected. These are the kinds of things we would want the boss to put in our record—if they were true, of course!

The appraisal should also be of us, comparing us with a standard that we have been told about. We'd like to know what is expected of us, We'd like to know, in specific terms, just what is considered a good job, then we'd like to be measured against that. We'd prefer not to be measured against the performance of another employee. After all, we were not hired to compete with other employees. We were hired to do a job that was described to us in enough detail that we could understand it and then trained to do it. It's upsetting when appraisal time comes around and we find that the standard has changed. It's no longer what we were told it was when we started. It's now the performance of one of the other employees. When we are told, "You aren't doing as well as Jake is doing on the same job," we have the right to ask, "Is that the standard?"

## FORMAL APPRAISAL SYSTEMS

After we've decided why we appraise and what we look for, we still have to know how to do the appraisal. There are different systems in different organizations. Many have a formal appraisal program. These are usually spelled out in detail in some kind of manual or procedures book, and supervisors are often given training programs on how to use the forms. There are advantages and disadvantages to having a formal plan. One of the strong advantages is that *it is done*. The plans usually call for doing appraisals at a certain time during the year, or require that they be done once a year for every employee, but not all at the same time. In either case at least an appraisal is done once a year, which is something that doesn't happen when there isn't a formal plan.

Under formal plans, there are usually provisions for doing a review of the job requirements or standards. This is done prior to the appraisal and usually includes a discussion with the employees being appraised. There are also forms to fill out while doing the actual appraisal. These forms include specific things to look for, and perhaps even a rating chart of some kind. The best forms do not have an "undefined" number chart, that is, a rating of one to five, but with no explanation as to what the numbers mean specifically. A good rating system will have behaviors defined, or at least some kind of standard to go by. There will be statements like "behavior occurs up to standard everytime the job is done" or "behavior is below standard more often than above it." Statements like these remove some of the guess work, though much is still left up to opinion or the supervisor's judgment. This is all right, since appraisals are basically matters of judgment anyway. Every effort is made to point out specific behaviors, and the more we can do this the better, but we have to realize that much of it is left up to our judgment in the end.

Some formal appraisals have the employees do a detailed appraisal of themselves at the same time the supervisor is evaluating them. The employees may be asked to outline their job duties as they see them, perhaps giving the standards from their own viewpoints and then a brief review of their perception of their performance over the appraisal period. The supervisor does this same thing and at a specified time the employee and supervisor sit down and go over the two appraisals together. The idea is to see if a match can be made, to clear up any midunderstanding and to reach agreement on the employee's performance. The process will work only if there can be some negotiation between the two. If the end product is just what the boss put down, then there's no point in the employees' going through their part of the exercise. If they feel their input is important, and that the boss will really let them have a chance to ask questions and give reasons for their point of view, then they'll spend enough time working on their part to make the system workable. Otherwise they'll catch on in a hurry and give us a meaningless piece of paper. This doesn't mean that we have to accept everything they say as right. It does mean that they will have a real say-so in what goes on their records. It also means—as we'll see later—that they received an explanation from us as to our evaluation of them.

Another advantage of formal appraisal systems is that they generally require a face-to-face interview with the employees being appraised. In times past, many appraisals were done without ever sharing the information with the employees. (In most places, now, personnel records are open to the employees and they have the right to look at any information at anytime they care to.) Even if the employees don't fill out any forms ahead of time, they still have an opportunity under this system to meet with the boss and go over their appraisals. That's not only a fair way of doing it, but makes the appraisal a much more helpful process. The supervisor has to defend what is written and the employee knows that there is accountability for behavior.

We mentioned that there are some disadvantages to a formal system, and here again, a little thought will show what they are. One, just the fact that it is formal tends to reduce it to "just one more step in the bureaucratic process of doing business." Supervisors remember it's time to do appraisals and they groan about it, put it off, then hurry through it without much thought. Of course, not everybody does it this way, but there is a tendency to think this way, since any kind of appraisal takes time. (Multiply the time it takes to do one appraisal by the number of employees we'll have working for us, and we can see how busy we're going to be doing them!) We have to decide if doing an appraisal in a hurry is better than not doing one at all, and the conclusion must be that it is, especially if there is some kind of interview required between the supervisor and the subordinates. Ideally, of course, we will choose to take our time and do the job right. This is the only fair way to treat our employees with any appraisal system.

Another disadvantage of formal appraisals is that because we do all of them at once, we can't help but make comparisons. As we appraise one person, consider the good and bad points carefully, measure the work in as much detail as possible, and come up with the best information we can comparing that person with the job standard, we then turn around and look at the next employee. What do we see? No matter how hard we try, we can't help but think about the first employee we appraised. We think about the two and then about how one does a certain job —not compared to the standard—but *compared to each other*. It's worse from then on. First we had one to compare with another, then two, then three, and so on. Pretty soon we're no longer comparing any of them with the job standard but with the other employees. It doesn't have to be this way, but if we aren't careful it can happen to us.

This is something we can try out on our own before we become a supervisor. We can look around at the people we work with and decide how we would appraise them. We know a lot about their jobs and what they're supposed to be doing. As we look at them, we can try to do a mental appraisal of them. We need to look at them one at a time, and decide how well each is doing in the job. Try to build an individual profile of their ability and performance, meaning that we don't just look at their *overall* performance, but at how they do on *each* of the things they are supposed to be doing. After we've done this on one person, go to the next and try it. See how long we can go before we start to compare one with the other. That's the test. We can do some practice on our own before making it to supervisor. We keep trying it until we get to where we can look at people objectively, comparing them to the job rather than to other workers. We can start on ourselves, by the way. See if we can objectively appraise ourselves without thinking in terms of the other people working around us. If we can go through

our whole job (all of the things we're supposed to be doing), thinking only of the job standards and not the others
around us, we're well on the way to developing skill in performance appraising.

One disadvantage we need to talk about is the fact that
since we know we are going to be talking to the employees
we appraise, we may tend to ease up on the criticism of
them. We may overlook some things that we feel, or not
mention them, since we never had brought them up before.
Or, at the other extreme, we may choose to really "lay down
the law" at appraisal time, criticizing things that we've let
pass and waiting for appraisal time to have a legitimate
chance to bring them up. Instead of dealing with the problems in performance as they arise—which is what we
should do—we let the employees go on doing the job incorrectly. There are all kinds of things that are wrong with
this, not the least of which is the unfairness of it.

Anytime there is a formal system for doing any job, a lot
of effort can get lost in the paperwork. Just think about how
it irritates us everytime somebody says, "Will you please fill
out these forms?" It doesn't matter whether it's for a fishing
license or for a mail order item. It seems to be something
designed to get in our way, rather than to move us along toward a desired goal. When we stop and think about it, we
realize that the paperwork is necessary. We know that busi-
nesses and service organizations have to keep records,
and that most of their operation runs on paper. In fact, if we
could examine it carefully, we'd find that most of it is necessary. The same is true of appraisals. There is a lot of paper
work, but most of it proves to be valuable in the long run. It's
just the *idea that we have to do it* that bothers us. It would
be good for us to prepare ourselves to accept paperwork
when we get to be supervisors, because it is a way of life.
When supervisors get called "glorified paper shufflers" the
name isn't a bad description!

## INFORMAL APPRAISALS

We've said a lot about formal appraisals because most organizations have such a plan, but we should say a few words about day-to-day, informal appraisals. There are several advantages to this kind of appraisal, and we should see how they work and how they should be done. The idea is that the supervisor constantly appraises his or her employees. It isn't seen as a once-a-year affair, but something that needs to be done all the time, with each employee. We would get awfully tired of our boss looking over our shoulders all day everyday, even if there were time enough to do it. The boss has more important things to do, of course. It would be impossible for him or her to observe everything we do, and give us an accurate critique. We aren't talking about the times when the boss has given us a significant assignment, explained the conditions and expectations, and then let us do the job after whatever training was necessary. At the end of that time, we are given some feedback on how well we did, what we did right and wrong. It may occur on the job site or in the boss's office, but wherever it is held, it will be what we're calling the informal appraisal.

In the informal appraisal, as with the formal process, many of the same rules apply. We want to be sure to tell the employees what they are supposed to be doing. They should know if they are being held accountable for their behavior on this particular assignment. They need to know what the standard for the job is. They ought to be told what they are seen as doing well and not so well. Enough direction should be given to them to let them see how they can improve. A time should be set up for them to be looked at again, after they've had a chance to work on improving themselves. (And by all means, we should be sure to do this follow-up!)

One of the best things about these informal appraisals is that they are less threatening than the formal ones. The session is casual, there is little or no paperwork involved, the employee doesn't have to do anything ahead of time to get ready for the session, and most often none of this goes on the record—unless there is some reason for documentation. Because of this lack of threat and the comfortable setting, it is much easier for the supervisor to "tell it like it is." This doesn't mean that it is done in a kidding way, or that the supervisor isn't serious about the things being talked about. It's just that the conversation can be very matter-of-fact, rather than stuffy and strained as formal interviews sometimes become.

One of the disadvantages of the informal appraisal is brought about by this unstrained atmosphere. Many times the supervisor will be so relaxed, the employees don't know they've had an appraisal. They aren't even sure the boss is serious, and because of the informality, they may not take it as seriously as they should. Even if they believe it, and recognize it as an appraisal, they may still not feel as much urgency to correct their behavior as they would with a formal appraisal. Another disadvantage is related to this one. The boss may do little in the way of preparation, since it is informal and casual. He or she may not do a very good job of analyzing the job to be done to determine a standard to measure against.

Finally, and perhaps the biggest drawback of all with the informal appraisal, is the fact that because there is no set time, no papers to fill out, and no accountability to higher management, many supervisors will just let the appraisals slip by without thinking about them. They simply won't have them. Other things will seem more important. Production will get behind or get rushed. New employees will need to be trained. There will be other reports to be filled out. The first thing we know, a year or two has gone by and there have not been any appraisals. The employees don't know how they stand; even the boss isn't sure. Then, suddenly the organization hurries to have appraisals of everybody, and there is mass movement of paper, with much too little thought put into getting very good appraisals. For a time there was nothing . . . then there is something that *may not be worth much.*


## SETTING JOB STANDARDS

The easiest way a supervisor can wreck a good employee and prevent a job from being done properly is by not informing employees of what they're supposed to be doing. The failure to set standards for performance is hazardous and unfair, yet is easy to do and many supervisors are guilty of it. Suppose someone were to ask our bosses what it is we're supposed to do. Would they get the same answer if they asked us? In some cases they would, in others they wouldn't. But suppose they asked our supervisors and then us how well we're supposed to do our job; would they get the same answers? Probably not, in most cases. Why is that? Mostly because setting standards is hard to do, and it takes time. It's much easier to set *responsibilities* than to set standards for those responsibilities. We can tell employees that they're supposed to greet customers, type letters, sell products, fix faulty apparatus, wait on tables, and on and on. These are all job responsibilities, not standards for doing them. When we discuss training, we'll see it's impossible to adequately train somebody if we don't know how well we want a job done. Think again of our own jobs: How well are they supposed to be done? Do we really know? If not, how can our boss appraise us? Many of us find out what the standard is by accident or by trial and error. We do the job a certain way, and if it pleases the boss, we decide we've done a good job (met the standard). If we don't please the boss, then we decide we missed it somewhere.

The hazard in this approach is that we may be only barely pleasing the boss, when we ought to be doing much more. We just don't know it. If we ask how well we're doing, our boss might reply, "Oh, fine," whatever that means. On the other hand, we may be doing an excellent job and not know it. When we ought to be getting recognition for a job well done, nothing happens, so that need isn't met, and we aren't as likely to continue doing the above average job without some kind of reinforcement. In the absence of a standard—stated by the boss and agreed upon by the employees—judgment of the performance may vary; hence, what we do one day that's pleasing to the boss may not be satisfactory the next.

## SETTING STANDARDS FOR THE JOB

Let's see what is involved when we talk about defining job standards. A job standard is just what the name implies: a standard by which performance can be measured. There is a standard, then there is performance by the employee. The two are matched together. If the performance isn't up to standard, obviously we have a below standard performer. If performance matches the standard, then we have an employee doing a satisfactory job. That sounds simple enough, but it isn't. It's a complicated process. Standards are hard to come by, difficult to prepare, and often hard to communicate to the employees.

There are some characteristics of good standards that ought to be mentioned. First, any standard that's going to be worth anything must be *realistic*. It must be "doable" in other words. It can't be something that sounds nice, but is a "pie-in-the-sky" dream that few employees will ever meet. It can't be the ideal when everything works right all the time, all the employees are trained perfectly, and all the employees have the full requirements for doing the job. It can't be that impossible dream that we are striving for but never really expecting to reach. On the other hand, it shouldn't be a bare minimum that is easy to meet but one that wouldn't really satisfy the job requirements if everybody met it.

A good standard should be one that is a reasonable expectation for an employee who is well trained and has the capacity of doing that assignment. It is prepared by looking at the job in the *absence* of any employees. We decide what we want and what is reasonable to expect. We look at the raw material, the equipment, or the money and time available, and decide that the kind of people we will be hiring for this job ought to be able to do this much. This becomes the standard. If we later find that actually the typical employee can do more or can't do as much, then we may change the standard. Note that we said the *typical* employee, not the above average, or the one who just isn't making it. We can't take the fastest, best trained, most ambitious, and most eager employee and set the standard for all the employees based on this one.

Next, the standard should be *measurable*. This is where it begins to get difficult to come up with good standards. Somehow we have to be able to take the job we're asking people to do, and put it into quantities and qualities that can be measured. Of course, some things are easily measured. If the employee is working on an assembly line, doing the same operation all the time, it's fairly easy to measure the production. We can measure sales-personnel by the amount of sales or kinds of items sold. We can measure people in service jobs by counting the number of service calls they make or the number of patients they see. These are the kind of jobs that make standard-setting easy.

Now let's talk about some of the more difficult standards to set. Just because a job is difficult to do, doesn't mean it is difficult to set a standard for it. Neither does the simplicity of the task make the standard easier to set. For example, take the simple matter of greeting a customer or a client. It may be a host or hostess job in a restaurant or a receptionist in a hospital. The job is one of greeting the customers in a manner that will give the organization a good image and make the people coming in feel comfortable. It is not a hard job, but hard to write a standard for. We immediately run into a problem of how to describe the person's action. Do we just say "pleasant?" Is that measurable? Would everybody seeing the person come up with the same feeling about whether the thing done was pleasant or not? Actually, no, because what is pleasant to one person might be boring to another, or even offensive. Imagine the difficulty we would have trying to tell a person that we will only be satisfied with them if they're pleasant, and then in answer to their question on what is the standard, we answer, "Well, pleasant is pleasant. Everybody knows what's pleasant and what isn't." Take it a step further and imagine that we're now in an appraisal interview with this person and we're trying to explain that there is a deficiency in pleasantness.

Us: So we've just got to do something about your not being pleasant to the people when they come in.

Them: Oh, I thought I was doing a pretty good job of being pleasant.

Us: No, that's the one thing I'm going to have to mark you down on.

Them: Well, just what is it I'm doing wrong?

Us: As I said, you're not pleasant enough.

Them:  How pleasant do you want me to be?

Us:  More pleasant than you are now.

Them:  How much more? A whole lot more? Just a little bit more?

Us:  I can't put a measure like that on it. It's just that we expect you to deal with the people in a more pleasant way.

Them:  I'll be glad to do whatever you tell me to do to improve, if you'll just tell me what you want.

Us:  Frankly, I think you're being obstinate about this. I'm beginning to worry about your attitude.

Them:  I'm sorry. I'm just trying to find out what it is you want me to do.

Us:  I told you several times, and I don't see how I can tell you anymore. Just do what you're told!

The conversation might not go exactly like that, but we can see the difficulty we would run into if we couldn't come up with a better definition of something that sounds as simple as "pleasant." In reality, we would begin to show some *behaviors* we wanted, such as more smiling, a change in the tone of our voice, the words we wanted used, and so on. We wouldn't try to measure "pleasantness" as much as the things that make a person pleasant. This gives us another characteristic of a good standard. Not only is it doable and measurable, but it also should be *observable* Not only should it be something that can be seen, but *seen the same* by everyone. Anybody observing the person performing, and having the standard, would see the same things happening. Whatever standard we set for being pleasant, for example, would be seen the same by everybody. If we wanted a smile, then everyone would see the smile and recognize it. If we expected the smile to be accompanied with a statement of good wishes for the time of day, anybody could see and hear it done up to standard.

Perhaps the best way to understand this matter of standards is for each of us to think about our own jobs and set some standards for parts of them. Try to pick something that's easily measurable and observable first and then go to something more difficult. We should try to find some part of our job that is not so easily measured or observed. Do we have a standard for that part of the job? What does the boss expect of us in this area? Could we come up with a standard that would meet the characteristics of good standards we've been talking about here? Would the boss be pleased with the standard we came up with? Would others be able to meet that standard? Are we meeting the standard we selected? This is a good exercise for us, because if we become a supervisor, we're going to have to do just these things. We're going to have to come up with standards for all of our employees on all of their activities, if we really want to be the best possible supervisor. We can practice now, both on ourselves and on the other employees around us. We can begin to try to think in terms of standards when we go into a restaurant, parking lot, or grocery store. We can ask ourselves, "What should be the standard for that job? What could I measure if I were doing an appraisal of that person doing that job?"

Let's put in a few words about *attitudes*. This is one thing that will get us into trouble very quickly if we aren't careful. When we do an appraisal, we may find that we don't have very good standards for a "good" attitude. If we confront an employee about an attitude, we may be in the same discussion we were in with the employee on the subject of being pleasant. Before we get in over our heads, we should try to decide what it is we mean when we say a person has a good or bad attitude. Again, we may find that there are certain actions that we like or don't like, and these determine our view of the person's attitude. If a person is coming in late, we may say that person has a bad attitude. Rather than deal with attitude, we'd be better off if we would deal with the behavior we don't like. We can observe a person coming in late; we can't observe an attitude. The same would be true for a good attitude. When we think of a person having a good attitude and start to describe it, we end up talking about things the person *does*: gets to work on time, is quick to take on a new assignment, likes a challenge, shares information with other employees, and so on. All of these things are observable, and we don't have to guess when we are telling the person in the appraisal interview what it is we like. (It's a little embarrassing when we are telling an employee we like their work, but not their attitude, and they reply, "Why don't you train me to smile. . . .")

## NO SURPRISES AT APPRAISAL TIME

No matter whether we find ourselves in an organization with a formal appraisal system or an informal one, we should promise ourselves right now that when we evaluate the performance of our employees, there won't be any surprises. What we mean by this is that we won't save up things to talk about until we get to the appraisal. Anytime we see an employee doing something consistently right or wrong, the employee should know it. There's no excuse for letting a poor job continue if we know about it. We should make the correction when we see it, or as soon as it is obvious that this isn't just a onetime action. If we feel this is the way an employee is going to perform regularly, we need to step in and bring it to the person's attention. Don't jump down the person's throat, but point out that the performance and the standards don't agree.

The same is true when we see that the employee's behavior on a certain job has been good; it's a good idea to reinforce that behavior if we'd like to see it continue. There's no reason to wait until appraisal time to deal with good behavior, though some supervisors like to do that so they'll have some good things to talk about to go along with the bad. This may soften the blow some, but here again, we have to wonder why they wait so long to talk about the bad things.

Some may wonder why we have appraisals if we are constantly talking to the employees about their behavior. We aren't suggesting that we are always telling them how they're doing, as we said earlier—looking over their shoulders—but we are watching for *patterns* of behavior. As we see patterns begin to develop, we don't want to wait to either discourage or encourage the behaviors we see. The reason for the appraisal is to set "benchmarks" where we can reference the employees behaviors up to certain points in time, and set up new directions if necessary. It is also a good time to get an accumulation of things we've said along the way. Because the appraisal is much more thorough than just our comments on the job, the employee gets a much better picture of our feelings about his or her performance. We can set some directions for development, and some time frames for review of the progress of this development.

## THE APPRAISAL INTERVIEW

We've stressed many times so far in this chapter the importance of having an interview with an employee as a key part of the appraisal. There are some specific things we need to know about an appraisal interview that will help us do a much better job of it. For example, the interview should occur at a time and place named ahead of time; it should not be a last minute thing in which we corner the employee in the coffee shop with, "By the way, you got a few minutes?" The purpose of the interview should also be made clear, so that the employees who are going to have their interviews will know the time, place, and purpose of the meeting we're having with them. It should be a pleasant time for both of us. We're going to be talking about the employee's growth and future in the organization. Under no circumstances should this turn into a disciplinary interview or even take on the characteristics of one. We want it made clear that we're going to talk about how each sees the performance of this employee (our viewpoint and that of the employee).

As we've already seen, ideally the employee will have been over the forms or the job descriptions beforehand, or will at least have thought about his or her performance before coming in for the interview. We will have done our homework, too, and we'll be familiar with this person's job responsibilities and performance over the *entire* appraisal period. We'll be keyed up for the interview. We'll feel like we're making a contribution to the employee's well-being. We're going to look at the future by drawing conclusions from past experiences and we're going to make that future work out well because we have a development program outlined.

Anytime we call a person in to talk to us, we have to realize there is bound to be a certain amount of stress generated. This means that we can't launch directly into the interview. We have to use some skill in putting the employee at ease. Maybe we could talk about the weather or the employee's family or some hobby. Anything to relax the individual. This shouldn't be long and drawn out, since the employee knows the purpose of the interview, but it should be long enough to break down any barriers to a successful appraisal session.

One thing we can do to make the employee comfortable and more at ease is to be sure that we haven't provided an uncomfortable place to sit—either a poor chair or a poor location. If the employee is having to look around a filing cabinet to see us or the chair is straight and rigid, we have some strikes against us already. The location of the meeting should be private, by all means. Remember we said that an appraisal is a very personal thing, so we want it to be just between us and the employee. If our office isn't private enough, we should make arrangements to go to a conference room or borrow somebody else's office.

Another cardinal rule about this interview is that it cannot appear to be hurried. If we don't think we'll have enough time, then we should put it off, delay something else or somehow make arrangements to have more time. Our problem is that we start thinking about how many interviews we have to have and start to hurry through them. It will help us to remember that no matter how many we're going to have, the individual employee is only going to have *one*. This person is concerned about just one future and that's the one being discussed in this interview. There's no way we can satisfy the employee by hurrying through it!

Once we've set the stage and put the employee at ease, we can start the interview. We should bear in mind that this is also a time to listen. It is to be a two-way exchange of information, aimed at getting mutual agreement on the performance of the individual being interviewed. We want to listen to what the employee has to say about his or her views of the performance, then we want to give our views, and we want to try to get agreement between the two views, if they happen to be different. As we mentioned earlier, the agreement shouldn't be forced. The employee shouldn't be forced to see our point of view, though we should have our facts in order so that what we say makes sense. We want to listen and then we want to talk. Our talking should be plain enough to be understood, and it should be documented well enough to be accepted as accurate. If we've done our job correctly, we'll not only have our views settled in our minds, but also have examples of behavior and performance to punctuate our statements.

Once we've presented our ideas and findings, we'll want to listen again. We'll never know if what we're saying is doing any good or being understood unless we get some feedback from the employee. This means that we may have to ask some questions, but not threatening ones, such as, "Don't you agree with that?" We will do much better with questions like "How do you feel about that?" There are questions called *open* questions that cannot be answered yes or no, and there are *closed* questions that can be. Note that the first question "Don't you agree with that?" is a closed question, forcing the employee to answer without being able to qualify the answer in any way. The other question is an open one, asking for a feeling rather than an agreement. From what is said about the feelings we can probably determine the person's agreement or disagreement. Of course, after the interview has been going on for awhile, and the employee is more relaxed, we can be more direct and get more firm information and answers. However, we should avoid direct, closed questions that start with the challenging word "Why . . .?"

Finally, this interview should end on a positive note. We don't want to avoid mentioning those below standard things that have been happening during the last period, but we don't want to stop with this as the last thing we've talked about. Rather, we want to end with a plan and with as much agreement as possible on the past and the future. We aren't talking about a promise of raises or promotions or anything we can't definitely see. We're talking about a plan that will be reviewed at a certain time and will have the employee on a track of satisfactory performance and development. And there will be a schedule for following up on this plan, *which will be our responsibility to keep.* The interview should be ended on a pleasant note, businesslike, but with enthusiasm to let the employee know that his or her interest is very important to us.

## USING THE APPRAISAL FOR TRAINING AND DEVELOPMENT

Part of the appraisal is to set some future goals and expectations. To get there may require some training. We will make a mistake if we don't tie the appraisal to the employees developmental needs. Where else will we get better information on what kind of training our employees need than from an appraisal? We have developed a profile on the individual and have found specific strengths and weaknesses. These weaknesses give us a perfect program for training and development. The employees will feel much better about going through training if they have seen it tied to their future during the appraisal interview.

We will have to set some priorities for which kind of training comes first. We'll have to decide what training will give the best and quickest results. We'll also have the problem of where the training will come from, who will do it, and how much time it will take. If we remember that the purpose of the training is to improve our employee, we'll work harder at establishing the training programs and finding the time for the training. It may be that not all of the training will come from the organization. We may suggest to the employees that they take some courses outside the job, do some self-development, use the tuition plan, or even invest their own funds in some additional education. We have to be extra careful, of course, not to make promises we can't fill. The training and development should be tied to the employees desire to be better, and our suggestions are for the purpose of showing the way. We shouldn't say, "This will get you a promotion and a raise." We should say, "If you want to do better in these areas of your job, here's what it will take on your part." We can also show what we're willing to do in the way of financial support for the education or what in-house training courses are available. We want a better employee and we'll come closer to achieving it if the employee also wants to be better.

## CONCLUSION

We've spent a lot of time talking about appraisals. We've talked about why we have them, what we look for in them and how to do them. Hopefully, we've left the reader with a desire to acquire this skill as soon as possible, even before becoming a supervisor. Some suggestions have been made along the way on how to begin to get these skills. There are some things we can do right on the job to increase our ability to appraise. We can look at ourselves, at our co-workers and get a real feel for the needs and problems of appraising. Perhaps the best thing we can do is to try to appraise ourselves as our boss would. Nobody is harder to understand than ourselves, so if we can succeed on ourselves, we've got a good chance on others!

# DISCUSSION QUESTIONS

1.   List reasons for doing appraisals.

2.   What are some of the things we look for in an appraisal?

3.   Discuss advantages and disadvantages of formal and informal appraisals.

4.   List some characteristics of good job standards. Then think about your own job and set some standards for parts of it. Consider the questions at the beginning of the chapter to help you assess your standards.

5.   What makes for a good appraisal interview?

6.   Try to appraise yourself as you think your boss would. What can you do with the results?

7.   How can we best use the information obtained from an appraisal? Where does training fit into this?

## chapter seven

# Supervisory Skills: Delegating

As we've said several times, the thing that separates us from our nonsupervisory job—when we make supervisor —is the fact that we no longer do the job; we get somebody else to do it. In other words, we delegate the work to somebody else. Thus we have another skill that has to be learned, and it's one of the survival skills. If we stop and think about it for a moment, we will begin to see the complexity we're about to face. There is something that needs to be done. The organization has decided that we aren't supposed to do it, but rather there are those under us who have it as their job to do. We have to go to them and say, "Here, you do this." That sounds simple enough, but think about it. Here's another human being, with a brain, with physical power, perhaps with a family and a car and bills to pay, and various problems that look just like ours, but the organization has made a distinction between us. It has said that one person does the work, another tells people to work, and the people involved are supposed to understand and accept the distinction. There may be very little else that is

different about them other than the assignment that the organization has given them. At one time we're on the receiving end, being told by others to do the work, then, when
we're promoted, we find ourselves on the giving end.
Though we may have aspired to this role for a long time,
when we get it, it may not be as simple as just telling employees to do the work. We have to learn how to delegate
the work in such a way that the employees will accept it, like
the role they're in, and keep coming back for more.


## WHY DELEGATE?

It may sound as if we're being repetitious when we ask
why delegate work, but we haven't fully answered that
question yet. The best way to understand why we delegate
is to imagine what would happen if we didn't delegate anything about the job. We can quickly see the chaos that
would develop. We can also see that our own job would become impossible very quickly. There's no way we could
keep up with all that needs to be done, and still do the
things *that have been delegated to us*. We would also have
to answer the questions of why do we need all those other
people if we're doing all the work? This sounds ridiculous,
but looking at supervisors now in the job, we may see that
many of them appear to be trying to do all the work themselves. As we watch them go about their jobs, they seem to
never let anything go; they keep all the information to themselves; they have people do things, then end up checking
all of the work. Listen to one of these supervisors giving an
assignment to a subordinate.

Boss:  . . . you understand what it is I want now?
  Sub:  Yes, sir. You want a report sent to accounting listing

our expenses for the month of June, using the form we used last month.

Boss: That's right. Nothing complicated, just a simple report. Uh, be sure to include the overtime. We've already got that figured out, haven't we?

Sub: Yes, sir. Unless it's changed since Thursday when we went over it.

Boss: No, it's still the same. We'll stick with those figures, I'm sure.

Sub: Anything else?

Boss: No, that about wraps it up. Unless you have any questions.

Sub: No, not that I can think of. Oh, yeah, I need to know when we need to get it to them?

Boss: We have to have it to them by Friday. That'll give them time to use the information for their overview by the first of the month.

Sub: Okay, I'll have it finished by Thursday afternoon, and get a couple of other things out of the way, too. I'll tag a copy to you.

Boss: Oh, well, uh, I, er, thought maybe I might need to look at if first. . . . Maybe you could finish it by Thursday morning. That way I could take a quick look at it, you know. Then if there were any changes to make, we could still get it to them by Friday. . . . How does that sound?

Sub: You mean you want to check over all the figures after I've done it.

Boss: Well, not all the figures. Maybe just a spot check here and there. I know you'll have everything right, so I'll just hit the old calculator a few times to make sure you haven't dropped a jot or tittle here and there. Ha, ha . . .

Sub: Yeah . . .

What did we find out? Has the boss delegated the assignment to the subordinate? What has been delegated? Has
the boss reduced his own work in the process of giving
work to the subordinate? These are the questions we have
to answer when we're talking about delegation. In this little
conversation we've seen many of the problems built in to
delegation. There's no question as to who is the boss. It's
not a question of authority to give the assignment, or special skills to get the job done. There's no question that the
subordinate understands the job and apparently knows
how to do it correctly. It isn't even that complicated, as we
understand from the conversation. Why did the boss delegate anything at all? From the subordinate's point of view, it
must be to get a lot of figures together so the boss can go
over them. What the subordinate really got was a lot of
work, with no real responsibility or authority. What the boss
got was a chance to duplicate work that a subordinate was
going to do.

This hypothetical conversation raises another question.
What about the motivation to do the job well? Think about
the times the boss has given us work that we know is going
to be checked and perhaps changed before it goes out.
Compare that with the times the boss has said, "When you
finish that, go ahead and send it out as it is. I won't get a
chance to check it, but I know you'll do it right." What's the
difference in these two ways of giving work to people?
Which is likely to get us the most motivated to do a good
job? The irony is that poor bosses think the first method is
much more likely to produce good work than the last one.
They'll say, "Why, if the employee knows I'm going to check
the work, it'll be done much better." But we know from our
experience that this isn't the case. If the boss has given
us a job to do, and expects us to get it right, and shows
enough confidence to let it go out without checking it, we'll
knock ourselves out trying to get it right. The smart boss

"Delegated his lunch to you and headed for Emile's Restaurant again, huh?"

knows this and uses it as a means of motivating us. But it's not a trick. It just makes sense that we all like to do things that we know how to do, and we like the thought of things going out of the work place with our name on them because *we did them.* On the other hand, we dislike the idea of somebody checking something after we've done the best we could—*and think we've done it correctly.*

This isn't to suggest that we delegate everything, regardless of the competency of the employees under us. People are not motivated when given a job they don't like or don't know how to do, and told it's theirs alone with no checking or follow-up. In the conversation we heard, we got the feeling that the subordinate understood the job, was able to do it, and was accepting the responsibility very well. Perhaps we even detected some enthusiasm. There was some planning being done. We can't help but feel that the job was going to be done well . . . up until the time the boss dropped a small bombshell: "That way I could take a quick look at it, you know. Then if there are any changes to make . . ." In other words, the subordinate *was not going to be responsible for the final product,* except the part that was right. Note that last phrase, "except the part that was right." If we don't delegate the *right to be wrong,* then we haven't fully delegated an assignment. What would the boss do if he found something wrong when he "hit the old calculator a few times?" He would change it, or get the subordinate to change it. What would he do if he found something right? He would let it go as is. As we've said, he would let only the right things go through, so the subordinate only had the right to be right, not wrong.

# AUTHORITY, RESPONSIBILITY, AND ACCOUNTABILITY

How can we make an issue out of letting things go out wrong? We don't want wrong things done, do we? What's so great about letting people make mistakes? Haven't we lost control and given up if we just say to people, "Do it any way you want to." No, and this kind of thinking—these kinds of questions—stems from a misunderstanding of delegation. We delegate to improve the end product, not make it worse. The idea is that we'll get a better end product if the employees are given some responsibility for the final results. We used the words "responsibility" but perhaps we should also use the word "accountability." People have mixed up their thinking trying to figure out the differences in authority, responsibility, and accountability. We don't have to solve the problem of their differences, but we can use them in a way to make it clear what we can and cannot delegate. There are those who say that we can't delegate the responsibility for a job that has been given to us. If our boss has given us a responsibility and we give the assignment to somebody else, we're still responsible for it—and that's right. So is our boss, and the boss above that one and the one above that one . . . and so on up the line. But if everybody is responsible, *then nobody is!* There is, however, an easy way to determine where the accountability lies. Just ask, "Who gets fired (or chewed out) if the job isn't done properly?" In most cases, it's the bottom person who gets it in the neck if things go wrong. (Unfortunately, at our level of first line supervision, "the buck stops with us" a lot of times, even though we've delegated it to somebody else. We'll talk about this and other hazards a little later in the chapter.)

To simplify, we can say that a person needs enough *au-*

*thority* to get the job done. By that we mean that we don't necessarily have to *delegate* the authority, but the subordinate has to get it in some way. Frequently, giving the person a job automatically gives the authority for carrying out the job. When the person says, "I'm responsible for the June budget figures now," the accounting department recognizes that the person also has the authority to ask for certain information. No letter or instructions are needed, other than credibility that the person really does have that responsibility. Of course, there are times when we will have to go through formal channels to see that the person has the necessary authority to handle an assignment. The right to sign certain letters, to approve amounts of money, or to get funds for travel may be acquired through a formal process of delegating authority.

Responsibility, on the other hand, is a matter of drawing a circle around a portion of work—including the amount of authority given—and telling the person just what the job is. Let's take another look at the case we heard earlier. After it was over, what was the subordinate responsible for? To tell, simply look at what the end product was. The job consisted of getting together figures for the June budget. These will be obtained from various sources, including some that had been worked on last Thursday (the overtime) and will be put on a form that is normally used each month. This information will be gathered, some calculations will be done, and then summarized. The summarizing apparently consists of nothing more than calculations which can be done by anybody familiar with the procedure. It seems the ideal kind of task that could be delegated to a subordinate. This is no doubt what the boss had in mind. But look what happened: That urge to check it before going out changed the entire nature of the assignment, from one of responsibility, accountability and authority, to one of only responsibility to gather information and to make one pass through it to get it in order for the boss to check it over. When it goes out, it will have the boss's stamp of approval—and we can always blame the boss if it's wrong!

## WHO GETS THE BLAME?

This brings us to another question about delegation: If something goes wrong, who gets the blame? We've already pointed out one way of testing this, and that's to find out who gets fired if things go wrong. But here we aren't talking about anything that drastic. We're really asking, if there's a question on the other end, after it leaves our work place, who do they come back to? If somebody doesn't understand the order, the piece of equipment is made wrong, or there is an error someplace, who does the user come to for help? We don't mean who gets the blame, we mean who helps the users out? Do they talk to the boss or the subordinate? Suppose they called the boss; what would the boss say? Would it be, "I checked that over, so I'll have to help you out on that," or does the boss say, "You'll have to check with my subordinate on that. It wasn't my job, so I can't help you." The ideal thing to be able to say here is, "My subordinate is responsible for that" and be able to say it in such a way that it's true. In other words, "I not only can't help you, but I'm not even the one who is *supposed* to help you!"

As we prepare ourselves to become a supervisor, we can think about this matter of delegation, and our own jobs. Look at the work we do. Are we really responsible for it? What happens to it when we're through? Does somebody else check it? What would happen if something needed correcting? What would the boss say and do? Is there a clear cut line in responsibility so that the boss couldn't help even if there were a need, because we handled the whole thing? Do we automatically check with the boss when we finish a job, even though we haven't been told to, or do we show him the final product only when asked to? Which method do we like best? Do we prefer to take the risk or do we like the security of having the boss in on it just in case there is a disaster? Perhaps finding the answer to these questions will teach us more about the true meaning of delegation than anything else we can do.

## HAZARDS OF DELEGATION

When we think about the security of having the boss share the responsibility and the blame, we're dealing with some of the real problems that arise in the use of delegation. This is especially true at the first level of supervision. Many organizations seem bent on finding somebody to blame for a mistake, even before correcting the mistake. If something has been delegated to us and we've had it all to ourselves, it's easy to see that there are some hazards involved. (It's comforting to have somebody else in the boat with us to bail, if it starts leaking badly! And if the boat is going to sink, it's nice to have a little company on the way down.) For this reason, we aren't always as ready to accept delegation as we might think. If we understand it in our present jobs, then when we become supervisors, we're more likely to understand some of the hesitancy of our subordinates to take the delegated jobs we offer. Lack of ambition may not be a factor. It may be that they've been burned a few times by handling something, only to have it come back in their face when things didn't go right. If we've experienced it, we can appreciate it, and even do something about it. We'll see what we can do to overcome this fear a little later.

Another hazard to delegation is the matter of how much protection to give somebody when we delegate to them. Let's imagine a situation where we have become a supervisor and have working for us a young woman who is capable of doing the job assigned to her. Gladys not only does the job well, but is eager to learn additional things about the job. We have given her some additional duties from time to time, along with the training on how to do them, and she's responded well. We finally reach a point where we aren't afraid to turn over entire operations, without checking her work. We do this in one particular area where she performed well in the past. We forget about it for several weeks until we get a call from our boss saying that there has been a mix-up with a client, and the client has gone to the big boss with a complaint. Our boss has been called on the carpet about the error, and is now charged with finding out how it happened and bringing back a full report.

What do we do? What should be taken back to the top boss? What should we report to Gladys? These are critical questions. Who's to blame? As we look into the matter, we find that the error really isn't too serious, and it is something we would have caught if we had continued to check. How much of this should be told to top management? Do we lay it on the line and suggest that the top boss be told that one of our employees goofed because we delegated the job and didn't check on her? Or do we cover up for the employee and take all the blame ourselves? How about the client, do we tell the whole story or merely that an employee goofed? Let's see some answers and reasons for the answers.

First of all, the client must come first, even ahead of the big boss. All this means is that we're in business to please clients, not big bosses! (Ideally, pleasing big bosses is pleasing the clients.) We also have to protect our employees, and if pleasing one client or customer ruins one of our good employees, we'll have to take a hard look at our choices. What does the big boss need to know about the operation or the causes of problems in the operation? The truth is, the higher up we go, the less detail the people need. Their job is planning and getting the organization staffed and organized in a way that the details can be handled far below them. Every time they concern themselves with information about things that happen at the lowest level in the organization, they're actually involving themselves *in somebody else's business*. They're probably neglecting a portion of their own job as well. The big boss needs only to know that the lower levels of management are aware of the problem and concerned about it. In almost every case, the mere fact that lower levels of supervision find out the problem from higher management is significant enough to create the concern.

That brings us to Gladys. We can imagine how she will take it if we inform her that the client has gone to the big boss with the problem, the big boss has passed it down to our boss, and our boss has asked us about it! We aren't going to have to spend a lot of time explaining to her the seriousness of the problem. In fact, the hazard is that she'll likely feel so badly that she'll want us to check everything she does from now on. We have to tell her about it and we can't play down the importance, but we can protect her from the bosses up the line. We don't have to put it in writing that Gladys is at fault and that she goofed because we let her have some responsibility. All top management needs to know is that we're taking action, we know where the problem is and things are being done to prevent it from happening again. We'll not be so bold as to say that it will never happen again. We make it clear that we're going to take care of the problem, because *that's our job*. When we turn to Gladys, we've got top management taken care of.

How we handle the problem with Gladys depends on

what happens when we discuss it with her—which we must do, of course. We don't call her in and chew her out. We simply point out the situation and ask her what she would recommend, after she's figured out how this problem came about in the first place. We can hope that she doesn't begin to make excuses, and she won't be as likely to if we approach it from a mature point of view. We should make it clear that we aren't trying to place blame, but to brace up a weak point in our operation. Also, we need to make it clear that she is a part of the strength that we'll use to do the bracing, not the weakness we're trying to overcome. Ideally, we'd like to see her analyze the problem, point out how and why it happened, then offer a solution to prevent it from happening again. We try to avoid the solution that gets us back to checking the problem area everytime work is done there. We agree to this only if we see that Gladys is really unsure of herself in the assignment and needs her confidence built up by some help on our part. Even if we agree to assist her for awhile, it ought to be only for *awhile* and *not permanently*. If she has shown she can do it, we ought to let her do it from now on, if at all possible.

Another hazard of delegation is that we may give an assignment to someone who doesn't want it or doesn't *deserve* it. We need to be careful when we're trying to motivate people with delegation, we don't want to force responsibility on people who aren't good employees or don't have much interest in developing. If we give a responsible job to somebody, it should be because they are willing, not because we think we can change their attitude by doing it. If we have somebody who is doing poorly, we don't give them more responsibility to change their actions, rather we offer the responsibility *if* they change their actions. Responsibility needs to be a reward for good action, not a means of overcoming undesirable performances. Closely akin to this hazard is having to "undelegate" work we've given to somebody. There is no ideal way of doing this, and it may be best simply to do it without much explanation and no apology. If we take work away from people because they're not handling it satisfactorily, that needs to be made clear. The problem is their unsatisfactory performance, not the taking away of an assignment. When we do take it away, we ought to make arrangements to reassign it to that person in the future when there is demonstrated competency. All this means is that we begin a training program immediately to raise the person's level of skill to where it will get the job done. If we have any questions in the beginning about the person's capability of handling the job, we ought to make the assignment not only temporary, but also point out that it's a training assignment that may go to several people over a period of time.

## LEARNING TO DELEGATE

How do we learn to delegate? The best answer is practice. As nonsupervisors, we have less opportunities to practice; however, we do have some. *We need to use them.* The best way to learn delegation in our position is to see what we're doing with our time now. We can learn to make good use of the time we have, and to do our work efficiently and orderly. We can practice some delegation even in our current job. For example, let's assume that at one time we handled a certain operation. Somebody else is now responsible for that operation, but people still call us for help or information. What do we do when somebody calls? Remember, since we once handled it, we know the answer, even though it isn't our job. We can do one of several things, not all of them helpful in learning delegation. We can give the information to the person, saving that person some time, getting the job handled quickly and efficiently, and building our own ego a little in the process. We can point out that this isn't our responsibility anymore and suggest the person not bother us anymore. Or we can give the caller the name and number of the person who now handles the operation, thereby getting them off our backs in the future. Which is best?

Let's go back and look at each possibility. First, we can do the job ourselves. Admittedly, this is the quickest way to handle it. The problem is that this simply postpones a problem, because the next time they want some information, guess who they call? Since they got help quickly from us before, why should they go somewhere else? So we've opened the door to being bothered from now on—or until we finally make the break with the job. We haven't learned much about delegation, though. Next, we can simply get out of it quickly by saying it isn't our job, and suggesting the person stop bothering us. This will keep the person from coming to us next time, but it won't give us much practice at delegating. If we try that when we become a supervisor, we may be in for a great deal of trouble! We haven't created much goodwill, and we've left the organization without a means of getting information. Finally, we can point out who is handling the work now, give the telephone number or location, and solve several problems. We've been helpful; we've moved the problem along to a solution; we've gotten the work off our back onto the rightful shoulders. We've learned something about delegation.

When we get to be supervisors, we'll still have to practice a lot to be good at it, and this includes learning how to handle paperwork and meetings. In the chapter on time management, we'll discuss how to make good use of our time and see the direct relationship between delegation and time usage. After all, we said that one of the reasons we delegated was to save ourselves some time. As nonsupervisors, it's interesting to watch our bosses at work, and see what they do with their time. The good ones may never appear to be busy. The ones who don't manage their time well may not get much done, but they always seem to be rushing around busily engaged in shuffling paper, going to meetings, talking on the telephone, checking on work in progress, and all kinds of things. In the end, they seem exhausted but don't have much to show for their efforts. The good delegator may never seem to be in a hurry, may not stir up much dust, but the end product is usually satisfactory, and the *quantity*, as well as the quality, is above average!

## BASIC RULES OF DELEGATION

We've talked a lot about delegation. Now let's summarize by looking at some of the basic rules:

Delegation is an area where learning can take place. One of the basic rules is that we should always ask ourselves "what learning do I want to take place as a result of this delegation?" If we go off and leave someone on a job to fill in for us it would be a much better learning experience if we have looked at certain things that we want the employee to try to improve on, work on, or experience while we are gone.

We always delegate to the lowest level of competency in the organization if possible. The reasons for this are obvious, but we need to remember that if there are those below us who can do work and do it almost as well as we can it's a poor use of time, talent and energy for it to be done at a higher level.

We don't always delegate to a person with the greatest ability. If delegation is going to be a training tool then we should give the assignment to people who need an opportunity to grow. While we don't want to go off and leave them untrained, yet accountable for a job at the same time, we will not produce much growth if we keep giving the assignment to someone who knows how to do it.

We do not delegate things that require our authority or level to accomplish. If there is some disciplinary action to be given or there is some praise to be handed out, we should not delegate that activity. If we are not willing to delegate the authority that goes with the assignment then we should not delegate the activity.

We don't delegate just boring or routine items. We need to resist the temptation to get rid of things that we don't like to do and keep the things that are fun. Since not much can be learned during the boring or routine activity, delegating them is not going to make it a learning experience. On the other hand if there is not much skill or competency required, we may want to make a permanent assignment out of the activity to some one lower in the organization.

We don't delegate things that involve safety, or could somehow prove to be dangerous to life or to the assignment. We need to accept that possibility ourselves and take care of those items rather than to delegate them.

Always determine the amount of authority needed to accomplish the task we are delegating and make sure that not only the employee knows that the authority has been delegated, but that other people who are involved will also have knowledge of this.

We need to identify the extent of the accountability being delegated. If we are going to hold the employee accountable for the final results, we should let them know this in advance, and that they will receive the credit for the good work that comes out of it.

One of the basic rules in delegation is to be careful not to delegate only the responsibility, but also the authority and accountability. If we do not supply the authority and let the accountability level be known, but still give employees the responsibility for the end product, what we have essentially done is to make an assignment for work, but nothing else. This means that there will be no recognition or sense of accomplishment, because when the final product is finished or the sound decision is ready, the employee will still have to come back to us for the authority.

## CONCLUSION

As would-be supervisors, we're going to have to learn to get out of work, as well as to learn how to work. We're also going to have to learn how to delegate work to others. We'll have to learn about responsibility, accountability, and authority, but we will succeed only if we understand the importance of getting the job done through other people. It's more than a phrase or a nice thing to do. It's a survival skill. There are some hazards involved, both to ourselves and the employees to whom we've delegated work. The risk is high, but the alternatives are worse. If we don't delegate, we'll have plenty to do, and this may not be good. When we're busy because we haven't learned how to delegate, we won't have time to notice all those people moving ahead of us!

## DISCUSSION QUESTIONS

1. List reasons why delegation is so important.
2. There are several questions to be answered in order for delegation to work, what are some of them?

3. Discuss the terms *authority, responsibility,* and *accountability* as they pertain to delegation.

4. What are some of the hazards of delegation?

5. If something goes wrong, how do we determine who gets the blame?

6. How do we learn to delegate?

7. We have seen that the best way to learn to delegate is to practice. Look for a specific situation in your job where you can do some delegating. Analyze your results carefully.

## chapter eight

# Supervisory Skills: Communicating

It's a bad thing to include a *separate* chapter in a book on the subject of communicating. The subject merits a chapter; the hazard is that it leads people to believe that communicating is a skill separate or apart from the other things done by a supervisor. For example, delegating is a skill. There are steps to do it, and we can do it or not do it. Training is a skill, and we'll talk about the steps in successful training in a later chapter. Appraising people is a skill and we either do it or don't do it. Are we suggesting that communicating isn't a skill? No, we're suggesting that it isn't something separate such as these things we've just mentioned. It's a skill, but we use this skill in doing these things we've been talking about. It's our tool for accomplishing them. When we delegate, we *communicate* the things we want done. When we train, we *communicate* the aspects of the job that need to be learned and then we *communicate* the proper ways of doing it. When we appraise, we *communicate* our findings to the person, and further *communicate* what we plan to do to see that the appraisal is even better

**151**

next time. In other words, we don't communicate as a separate part of the job, but *we communicate while we're doing
the job.*

Making a separate chapter on communicating is doing
something we can't do on the job. We can't separate communicating from the job. When we answer the telephone,
we're getting ready to communicate; when we call an employee in for a disciplinary session, we're getting ready to
communicate; when we hold a meeting, write a letter, or go
see the boss, we're going to engage in some communicating even though we may not call it that. Then why have a
separate chapter? Because by isolating it, we are able to
call attention to it and still apply its use to these other things
we've been talking about. We'll try to see what communicating and how it relates to the day-to-day activities.

## WHAT IS COMMUNICATING?

Whatever else we can say about it, communicating includes getting a message from one place to another. It can
take many forms. We can shake our first and get a message to someone. We can write a love poem and one dear
to us will get a special message. We can wire money with
no comment, and the college student gets the message immediately. We can write a short memo or a long report and
somebody will get some kind of message. We can call a
conference or make a public speech and the attendants
will get something from it. All of this comes under the heading of communicating. We have neither the time nor the in-
clination to get into poetry writing, money wiring, or fist
shaking, but we do need to learn about writing and speaking if we're going to be supervisors someday.

Notice that in our definition we haven't said that the message got there exactly as we wanted it to. That comes under the definition of "good" communicating. In fact, we can define good communicating as getting a *specific, predetermined* message from one place to another. All that says is that we got the intended message across to the person we wanted to receive it. That's not easy, as we'll see, especially since we often have the disadvantage of not being able to pinpoint the problem of unsuccessful communicating. Since at least two people are involved, we can always blame the other party (even though they may be blaming us). What we want to do in this chapter is to define the elements of any communicating effort, and then find out what we can do when we become supervisors to improve the skill.

# ELEMENTS OF COMMUNICATING

It helps to understand communicating if we break it down into its basic elements. First, there is the person who has a message to send. We call this person the *sender*. Where does the message come from? From the sender, of course, but how did the sender get it? Usually it was first an idea in the mind of a person, then there was a desire to transmit that idea to someone else—either one person or a group of people—and next there was the putting of that idea into words of some form. It may have been spoken or written. It may have been well thought out or only half-baked. The sender has the responsibility of the *encoding* of the idea into words, since words are simply the codes we use to get an idea from one brain to another. The idea may have been to explain a complex process or a simple concept. We may have wanted to teach a person how to write a computer program or simply to tell a person what time we will eat. In either case, it started with the idea, the desire to express that idea and the putting of the message into words, either written or spoken.

The next element is the *message* itself. As we've said, it may be only half-baked, that is, only half put together, or it may be in very precise language. It may still not do the job, if the preciseness is that of the sender and not of the person to whom the message is intended. The college professor may be very precise in words and fail to communicate with the farmer who has spent a lifetime in the fields, not in the classroom. The reverse would probably be equally true, with the farmer trying to send a message to the professor. Anytime we send a message, it represents a *part of us*. It comprises some of our background, our experiences, our prejudices and biases. It certainly consists of our language and word meanings. When we choose a word it is generally a word that means something to us. It's a word or group of words that best describes to *us* the things we're thinking about and want to transmit. If we're good at communicating, we'll take the time to decide whether that word means the same thing to the person we're sending the message to. One of the problems we have is that from early childhood we are led to believe that words have specific meanings to everybody. We think of the dictionary as being the rule or guide for the precise meanings. Actually, it's not so important that words have meanings. What is important is that *people have meanings for words*. This is where the uncertainty and confusion often arise. Different people have different meanings for the same words, as a result of their upbringing, their experiences, and even the part of the country they come from. This creates a problem in communicating since we can't always tell what meanings people will have for the words we want to use. They may "understand," but in their own context arrive at quite a different meaning from ours.

Another element is the *receiver*, of course. That's the

person to whom we want to get the message we've thought up and encoded into some form. Even within our own family we know that everybody has a little different background, different experiences, different friends. Perhaps they don't have the same desire to get the message as we have to send it. They may desire to get it but aren't willing to spend undue time working on the *decoding*. They'll take the first meaning that occurs to them without working at it. And they may end up misunderstanding what we've said!

For the sender to be successful, there must be an understanding of the receiver's needs, motivation, background, and interest in the subject matter being transmitted. Obviously this isn't possible, so we resort to other ways to guarantee success. Since we may not know a particular person, we can at least try to figure out the background of the person we're talking to. Are we talking to a person whose background is likely to be mostly union oriented, from the farm, or someone who has grown up in a large city? If we know this much we can predict a few things we need to know about the receiver's possible interests and needs. Admittedly, we can make some mistakes this way, but at least we have a better chance of success than we would have if we knew nothing about the person. There are other ways, but we'll talk about them a little later when we talk about *feedback*.

One more element of the communicating activity is the *media* or means of sending the message from the sender to the receiver. It may be that we simply tell a person something we want them to know. At another time, we may choose to send a letter or a memorandum. There is the telephone or telegram, or even a third party, where we tell one person to tell another one something for us. Each of these is a little different from the other. Telling somebody depends on a good first-time effort, since it can't be "reheard" as a letter can be reread. Usually a memo is less formal and may contain less information. It may even be easier to understand *because it is shorter.* Telling a third person to tell somebody something is obviously dangerous, and we can rightfully worry about whether or not the message gets there. In fact, we aren't certain until we see some action from the intended receiver, or receive some feedback that indicates the message was properly transmitted and received.

This brings us to the final element we want to talk about: The *situation* under which the message is sent. There has always been something urgent about a telegram, and if we're expecting big news of some kind, we may be frightened, excited, or awed by getting a telegram. If we're expecting to hear from someone in a high position, and the message comes on a printed form or in a very informal memorandum, there is a letdown. On the other hand, if we are waiting anxiously for news and aren't sure whether it will be what we are hoping to hear or not, any way it comes will be all right so long as we hear the right thing. When we become a supervisor, it won't matter whether we read it in a memo, hear it on the telephone, or even from a third party. We'd like, however, for it to be authentic when we hear it. Did the message come from a source that is reliable? Is it based on rumor or fact? If we have to confirm the accuracy of the message, we are less likely to listen to rumors than if we don't have to have the data verified. That's why rumors spread so quickly in an organization. They don't have to be verified, so they can travel at high speed, gaining both in speed and unsubstantiated facts.

## THE NECESSITY OF FEEDBACK

No matter what message we're sending, who we're sending it to, or what means we're using to transmit it, we cannot communicate successfully if we ignore the need for *feed-back*. Feedback, is simply hearing or seeing something to indicate what message was received at the other end. In an ordinary conversation it's easy to get feedback, *if we learn to listen*. Frequently we don't bother to listen, spending all our time either talking or thinking about what we're going to say when it's our time to talk again. When we write a message, the feedback is delayed; we have to wait for the results of the message to show up in some kind of action, such as an answer to our letter. Good communicators build in some guarantees for getting feedback. They'll ask specific questions or indicate a specific action that will tell them that the message got through. "Call me and give me the exact number you'll need" may be all that's necessary to see whether the person understood the order. "I'll look for the announcement of the meeting as soon as you decide the date and time," may tell us whether the message is understood by the person taking the chairperson role of the newly formed committee.

Consider the things that good communicators have in common. If we think about our experiences with people who are good at getting messages across and understanding what others are telling them, we may see them in the following description. First, we find that good communicators *know the message* they're getting ready to send. This doesn't mean that they are experts on the subject. While that may or may not be true of them, one thing is certain about them: When they start to say something, they've decided just what it is they're planning to say. They don't start off with a half-finished idea and make it up as they go. If they call somebody on the telephone, they're ready to talk when the person answers. They have the letter on hand they want to discuss; they have the figures underlined where they think there is a discrepancy; they're ready to deal with the subject at hand. They don't start off by saying,

"I wanted to talk to you about this letter I just received. I, uh, had a question or two about it . . . let's see now, I think it was in the first paragraph, uh, hmm, no, maybe it was the second paragraph. . . ."

The same would be true whether we were writing a letter, talking on the phone or sitting across the desk from someone. Communicating is a skill that can be learned. It's a habit we can get into, saying to ourselves, "Just what is the reason for this particular communicating effort?" We don't have to have the whole thing planned, but we ought to have at least the first few thoughts put together, and the overall purpose of the transaction.

The second thing good communicators have in common is that in addition to knowing the message, they *know the message got there*. They practice feedback gathering we mentioned earlier. People do it differently. Some will take all the responsibility on themselves for any misunderstanding by saying something like, "Just to make sure I'm saying what I intend to, how about giving me a rundown on what I said." Another may put the responsibility on the listener or the receiver by saying, "Let's make sure you got the message. How do you interpret what I've been saying?" Someone else might check feedback by seeking to find out what action is going to be taken as a result of the communicating. "Based on what I've said so far, what's going to be your first step?" Others will get the feedback in other ways, but they're all aiming at the same goal: checking to see if their message got there.

A final thing—and by far the most important, as we'll see—good communicators have in common is the skill of listening. We need to distinguish between *being quiet and listening*. Many people confuse the two. The real communicator listens for all kinds of things, realizing that only through good listening can we find out the between-the-lines meanings, the specific points of objections, the steps

"Actually, I doubt Janet will ever make it to our level — notice how her employees seem to understand everything she says?"

we're expected to follow and so on. Some of us think that just because we're not saying anything, we're listening. We can check ourselves easily. The next time we're talking to someone, see how often we interrupt before a complete thought is finished. We can see how many times the person has to repeat something because we didn't get the whole idea the first time, and how often this was the result of our not listening the first time.

Now let's see why listening is so important. First, it's hard to do, it's hard to learn, and it's *easy to forget*. The most distressing thing of all is that we never become so good that listening becomes effortless. It's not a natural reaction. Most of us would rather talk than listen. No matter how good we are at it at any given time, we can lose the skill very easily. When we think we're good at listening and quit thinking about it, we lose it again. The reasons for listening are obvious, as we've already seen; not only do we need to listen to determine what a person is saying, but to acquire the *feedback* whenever we're talking to somebody. How can we know what the person is receiving from us if we don't know how to listen. Once we lose the skill of listening, we're totally dependent on our own efforts at getting the message across. We have no opportunity for correcting what we've said, trying a different approach, or using another illustration for clarity. If we think we don't need to know how to listen, then we're completely confident in our own ability to get the message across the first time. Not many people will admit to being that good!

## COMMUNICATING TO GROUPS

What we've been talking about so far is communicating in general, regardless of what method we're using. There will be times when we will have to stand before a group and give a speech. That's a very difficult form of communicating. Aside from stage fright that sometimes bothers us, it's virtually impossible to use all the things we've been talking about here. We cannot speak on the level of every person in the audience. We won't be able to *find out* the level of everybody, no matter how much time we have. Also, there's the problem of the lack of feedback. We can receive general impressions of how our message(s) is (are) being received, and maybe a few comments that will give us feedback, but this is far from the kind of feedback we can get when we're talking to someone face-to-face.

There are some things we can do to improve our communicating efforts in front of a group. First, we can admit to ourselves that it is a difficult task. This will put us on guard and automatically increase our sense of urgency to watch for signs of problems. We can pick words below the level of the average of the group, as we expect them to be. We can give more than one illustration or example, if the group has a mixed background. We can have some feedback exercises, asking for questions, asking questions ourselves, making it clear we aren't trying to put anybody on the spot, but just trying to see how well we're getting our message across. We can watch for signs of disagreement or watch for puzzled expressions. It's perfectly acceptable, in fact preferable, to stop and say, "I think I'm getting a message from the looks on your faces that you aren't sure just what it is I'm saying. Am I reading you right?" Of course, we have to be careful when we're reading faces, because that's like reading minds: *pretty hazardous* and highly inaccurate. Listen for feedback, though, and we'll find out how accurate we are.

# COMMUNICATING IN WRITING

Just as we aren't going to give a complete course in public speaking, we can't go into letter writing in any detail. We can, however, point out some of the difficulties in communicating this way and some of the ways of overcoming them. If we were to rank ways of communicating in the order from easiest to hardest, we'd most likely say that talking directly to one person is the easiest. The person sees us, hears our words and the tones we use, and we see and hear their reactions. Next comes talking to somebody on the telephone, since we still have the advantage of getting feedback from them, and they can hear our inflections. We miss being able to see their faces, and they can't see our gestures (though most of us still use them when we're talking on the phone). Talking before a group is next, since they can see and hear us, though we can only see them and their reactions and not get feedback from each one. Finally the worst form of communicating is writing. The receiver can neither see us nor hear us; we can say only a few words in a letter. When we realize that a one-page, single-spaced letter represents only a little over a minute of communicating, we see that it would take a lot of writing to say very much—compared to talking on the phone or face-to-face. To add to the dilemma, we get absolutely no feedback at the time of the writing. It's only when we get a response or see some action that we are able to know how our message was received, and then it may be too late.

All of this says that writing presents hazards to getting messages across, it should be done very carefully, and with expectations of not being completely successful. Armed with this philosophy, we'll be better supervisors when it comes to writing. Everytime we put something in writing we will tell ourselves, "Watch out! They may not get the message." Then we go out and do our best to get the message across in writing. Let's look at some rules of writing that will help us be more successful.

First, as in any communicating effort, we should decide just why we are writing in the first place. If we mentally give ourselves a reason for writing, we'll more likely say what we want to say. The next thing is to decide exactly what we want to say. The way to handle this is to ask ourselves, "If the person only understood one thing from reading this, what would I want it to be?" When we've finished the letter, we reread it and decide if this one fact is presented so that the reader will actually understand. If we did this more often, we might write to the point with fewer tangents.

This brings us to the next point to remember. *Stay on the subject.* As simple as this sounds, we still will find ourselves adding clauses, putting in things that we think will help the understanding, but actually draws attention away from the subject at hand. The trick is to come up with short sentences, simple words, paragraphs limited to just one idea, and letters addressing one subject if possible. For some reason, people sometimes get the idea that a good letter is one that has a lot of commas and complex sentences, sprinkled with those meaningless expressions such as "pursuant to . . ." and "with proclivity and haste. . . ."

There are some other basic rules we should mention. For example, it's a good idea to begin the letter with the purpose stated in the first paragraph and first sentence if possible. If we want the person to do something, we should make sure that it is in the first paragraph and the last, since we know that people remember the first and last things they read, and very little of what is in the middle of the letter. We also know that people are more likely to read a letter more carefully if it's only one page long. They're also more likely to read short ones first, putting the long ones aside until they have more time. When we put these rules together, we have a good picture of the kind of letter that will be the most effective. Finally, most people have trouble closing a letter. For that reason, they end up using such ridiculous expressions as, "If we can be of further help to you in this or any other matter, please do not hesitate to call on us." Because it is used so much, it is now considered unfriendly and not in the least personal, although most people who use it are trying to be just that. The best way to end a letter is to stop when we've said what it is we wanted to say. If we've answered a question, given information, or asked for help, and all is understandable, then we should just close and sign the letter. That's a polite and friendly way to do it.

## CONCLUSION

We have seen that communicating is difficult and that there are some things we can learn to improve the skill. In summary, we should recognize that words are just codes and as we send codes, the people at the other end may not understand the codes we're using. For this reason, we will need to get feedback. This is best accomplished by listening—a skill that's hard to learn and easy to lose. Even though it's difficult to get a message across, even when we're talking to one person, this is the easiest form of communicating; as opposed to, speaking before a group, talking on the telephone, or writing to somebody. Whatever form we're using is going to be better if we realize the hazards involved and work at improving them. We can learn a lot about communicating before becoming a supervisor, since we're communicating with people all the time. This is an advantage to us, since we need to be good at it as soon as we become a supervisor. It's a survival skill—since it's the tool we use to delegate, appraise, and train. If we think we have something to say, it's a shame to lose the message because we can't communicate very well!

# DISCUSSION QUESTIONS

1. What does good communicating consist of?
2. Consider the traits that make a good communicator.
3. What are some rules we can follow in order to improve communicating in front of a group?
4. List some rules of writing that will help us to be more successful in our communicating.
5. Discuss the importance of feedback in any form of communicating.

## chapter nine

# Supervisory Skills: Training

Of all the survival skills needed by the newly promoted supervisor, the ability to train correctly and quickly is perhaps the one with the most pay-off. Remember that we said we can't appraise somebody fairly if we haven't trained them ahead of time. We found that we couldn't expect them to accept delegation unless we had made sure that they knew how to do the job. We saw that responsibility and recognition were good motivations, but if the employees don't know how to do what it is we're trying to get them recognition for, then we've failed in that mission completely. Altogether, this says that training comes first—and that's exactly right. We just have to think about the frustrations that have come to us in the past when we were left with a job that had to be done correctly, but nobody had told us or showed us how to do it. We hadn't been trained. When we become a supervisor, we can avoid having our employees feeling that way by properly training them. In this chapter we'll mention some of the ways to train effectively and efficiently.

# WHY DO WE TRAIN?

As obvious as it seems, and as much as we've said about training, it still is important that we understand why we train our employees. Think of the job that we have now. How much of it did we learn on our own, how much from formal training, and how much from watching others or by trial and error. As we think about it, we discover that a large amount of it came to us in ways other than *formal training*. This sounds like a good argument *against* training, since we think we're doing fairly well. Is it? Not really, when we realize how much time has been wasted by us in doing things over, and by others in correcting our errors. But wait, somebody says, isn't experience the best teacher and don't we learn more quickly when we're thrown in over our heads? These are platitudes fostered by ineffective supervisors who have stayed alive by having luck and people under them who learned fast enough to keep them out of trouble in spite of the poor training being done! There's no question that many people have learned a lot by being thrown in over their heads, but perhaps an equal amount have nearly drowned and have had to be pulled out and given another job or more training.

Experience, like practice, makes us perfect only if we're doing the right thing. Many of us do things wrong day-in and day-out, simply because we learned incorrectly in the first place—perhaps trying to swim on our own—and never having unlearned the bad habits. If we had initially been trained properly, we would have learned the correct procedures and never known the wrong way. There are always those around us who have been on the job for many years and received little formal training. They are often the first to ridicule any training effort. Unfortunately, some of those are supervisors, and they fight training as though it were some kind of evil or dread disease. A little reasoning will show that training is important, though there are many things we can and do learn on the job without training. If we are assigned to do a job and there is a specific way of doing it—some kind of standard—what possible justification can there be for keeping this standard from us? The sooner we learn the standard and are trained to accomplish it easily and efficiently, the quicker the boss can turn us loose and go on to some other task; we can be left alone with confidence. We can begin to get some of that recognition and be given some of that responsibility that is so important in motivating us to do our jobs without supervision.

## WHAT DO WE TRAIN FOR?

It is equally obvious that we can't be trained for everything there is to do on the job. When we become supervisors, we'll have to stop somewhere. Where do we stop? Is there some kind of rule of thumb? Yes, and it goes back to survival again. The basic rule is to train people first for those things that are vital to the job, that will protect the equipment and the employee from harm. We find those things the employee knows absolutely nothing about and start with them, if they are vital parts of the operation. We divide the job into "have to know now," "have to know soon," and "have to know one of these days." The have-to-know-nows are those that mean nothing can be done at all until they are learned, the employee can blow up the plant by doing them incorrectly, cut off a hand by doing the wrong things, or turn away a customer with an improper word.

We can postpone training until the employee is ready to do the new work, and we can avoid some training by determining what the employee can already do. We don't want to get into the habit of training just for trainings sake, regardless of whether or not the employee needs it or will ever be doing the procedure. For those things that take practice, basic training is followed by supervision of the work. When we first become supervisors, most of the people who will be working for us will already have been trained, for the most part, so our job will be easier. Fortunately, we won't immediately have to train everybody. We'll have a chance to practice one or more of the other skills we've discussed before we begin training. We'll also have a chance to look at the people and make some decisions about what kind of training they need before we begin.

The ideal situation for a new supervisor is to train a person for those things that he or she does frequently or that aren't being done correctly. We can start on that right now by looking at ourselves and deciding what kind of training we need. If we were our bosses, what kind of training would we decide *we* need to do our present job. No matter how good we may be, there are always areas where some things aren't being done as they should be. There is a standard and we aren't meeting it. If the reason is we don't know how, then training is the answer. We can also look around us and see what kind of training others need. Pick some of the people we're working with and imagine that they work for us. As we look at their performance we see some things that aren't as good as they are supposed to be, as far as meeting standards are concerned. We ask ourselves, "Would training help?" If we decide that it would, then we have the beginnings of a training program.

If we want to really grow in this area, we will take it a step further and determine *why* we decided training was needed and would make a difference in the employees' performance. This is what we're going to have to do when we become a supervisor, so let's practice now. There are some questions we can ask about the people we're looking at. Suppose their jobs depended on doing the job correctly; could they perform up to standard right now? If the answer is yes, then training isn't the solution to overcoming poor performance. One of the ways we can tell if they could do it if their jobs depended on it, is to ask if they've *ever* done it correctly, or if they occasionally do it right and occasionally do it wrong. If this is the case, then it may be that they just don't know when they're doing it right and when they're doing it wrong; so again, training isn't the answer. The answer may lie in lack of motivation, lack of feedback from the supervisor on what is correct, or lack of reinforcement when the job is done correctly.

## SETTING STANDARDS FOR THE JOB

We can get more practice for the training job we will have as a supervisor if we acquire the habit of thinking about *standards of performance*. The only way we'll ever be successful as trainers is to teach a standard. The only way we are able to know if an employee is below standard is to have a standard, and the only way we'll know if we've been successful in our training efforts is to see whether the employee can now meet that standard.

Setting standards, however, isn't easy. Think about it in our present job. Just what is the standard? How well are we supposed to be doing? Do we know that definitely, or do we just *think* that's the standard? As we look around us, what are the standards for the others working with us? Do they know what it is they're supposed to be doing *and how well?* It takes more than just knowing what our *responsibility* is. We need to know the quality or quantity of work that's expected of us. What is a standard? Some believe it is that which we would like to see people doing, although we know that very few will ever reach that goal. Others think a standard is that which most people in a particular job do, or the average of all those who perform a similar task. Still others think of it as being what the best employee is doing—a target for all the rest to shoot for. None of these are a good definition of a standard. A standard is a reasonable expectation of anybody performing in this job, if it can be assumed that he or she has the basic talent to do the work. Once it is set, then it becomes the standard, and it is the standard for everybody doing that job. It must be measurable and observable. We can't say that the employee is to be "efficient" or to "please the customers." Remember, when we do an appraisal of the person (which is a measure of performance against a set standard), we'll want to be able to speak in *specific* terms, not generalities.

## STEPS IN DOING THE TRAINING

There are some specific steps in doing successful training, and we need to look at them. Good training isn't accidental or a matter of luck. Training is good because we decide what the standard is and then use good methods of training so that the employee will meet this standard. There are some *right ways* to train, just as there are some wrong ways. Let's see what some of those right ways are.

First, let's set up some "standards" for training, since we've been talking about standards for doing any job. Training is successful only if we're able to get the employee involved. People remember the things they've heard or seen better if they've been involved in some kind of activity. The training we do, then, must involve the employees as much as possible. It's fine if we tell them or show them something, but it's going to be wasted—for the most part —if we don't get them involved. They will remember what

| We Tell | Employee Tells | Employee Tells |
|---------|----------------|----------------|
| What | What | What |
| How | How | How |
| Why | Why | Why |
| WE DO | WE DO | EMPLOYEE DOES |
| | | EMPLOYEE PRACTICES |

**Figure 9.1 Steps in successful on-the-job training**

they say much longer than what we say, and they'll remember what they do much longer than what we do. The ideal training includes employees involvement along with the activity of the trainer, as we'll see in a minute.

Next, we must know what the employee is thinking and what the employee is able to do, we find this out by getting feedback. In other words, we hear the employee talk about the steps and reasons for precautions and expected results, and we watch the employee perform so we'll know just what part of the skill is getting through to become action. We may be able to tell, but we want to hear the employee tell us. We may show them, but we want to see the employee do the thing we're showing. This kind of feedback will enable us to not only evaluate the employee's ability, but our own ability as trainers.

Now, let's look at some specific steps in successful training. We'll refer to Figure 9.1 for this part of the discussion. The top part is what is being said, and the bottom part is what is being done. It also tells us who is talking (or telling) and who is showing (or doing). A primary rule is that no one does anything until the telling is said correctly. The horizon-

"As a last resort, we have two choices — arson or training."

tal line in the middle is called the "life line." It protects the employee and the equipment. If the telling is done correctly, then we can go below the line. If the telling is incorrect, then we go back and correct it, before going any further. If we train properly, we'll get the information in the employee's head before getting it into the hand!

The first step is for us to tell, then for us to do. Next, we have the employee tell—and if the telling is correct—we perform or we do, as can be seen in Figure 9.1. Next, we have the employee tell, and if it's told correctly, we let the employee do. These three steps are simple enough, and they will produce great results if we follow them carefully. Let's consider some things about the telling. One thing we must remember is that we only tell those things we want the employee to tell us. This means that we will avoid going into long histories of how the equipment used to look, how it used to be done, and how it was in the "good old days." (Unless we want the employee to tell us this in return.) Specifically, we tell *what* it is we want done. Then we have the employee tell us the same thing. If it's important, we tell *how* it is to be done. We give the step-by-step processes and procedures, remembering that we want the employee to tell us these things before any action will be allowed on his or her part. Finally, we tell *why* it is done in these specific ways, if why is important. If there are safety reasons, then we want to explain them, and we want to hear the employee tell us these same safety considerations. If there is a possibility of damaging the equipment or losing a customer by doing it incorrectly, we not only want the employee to know it, we want to hear the employee tell us about these considerations.

## THE JOB OF FOLLOW-UP

When we are through with the initial training, following the rules and procedures we've just discussed, our job still isn't finished. If we remember the early training we received, when everything seemed to run together and was confusing, we thought we would never be able to remember all the things we were supposed to do. We wouldn't have, either, if there hadn't been a chance to practice and to follow-up. Imagine how it would have been if our boss had given us the training and then disappeared. That has probably happened to some of us occasionally, and it's frightening to be left alone without having complete confidence in ourselves that we know the job completely. This doesn't mean that we have to be spoon-fed or have our hands held every step of the way. We merely want to have a chance to practice under somebody who knows the job and can correct any mistakes we make when we start doing the job. All of this is called follow-up. We want to do it when we get to be supervisors, so that our training will be as effective as possible.

This doesn't mean that we aren't willing to let the employees work on their own, or that we don't trust them. It simply means that we want them to have the advantage of our best training effort, so after we've trained them, we do some periodic follow-up to make sure that the training isn't lost. We can think of it as a sharpening up process. Our first effort —no matter how good we were—will get lost if there isn't some kind of reinforcement along the way. Ideally, the employee will be involved in the task immediately after the training. Being able to apply what we've learned soon after the training is one of the best ways to retain the information. As we practice, the skill gets sharper and becomes more of a habit. When we've trained an employee using the method described, we know that the employee's thinking process regarding the operation is correct. As we see the employee performing on the job, we know that the skill is being done correctly. After a little observation, we can forget about the employee for awhile, as far as this skill is concerned, because we have good evidence that the employee not only knows how to do the job but can do it. That's our reason for training in the first place!

## CONCLUSION

Here are several reasons that are often given for training: the employees expect it, we have the time, we've always trained the employees, and the employees have a bad attitude—all of which are the wrong reasons for training. We train because the employees can't do a job we expect them to do. We train when—and only when—there is a standard and the employees aren't meeting that standard. Even then, we only train if we are sure that training is the best solution to the problem. We do not train if the employee can actually do the job, but for some reason isn't doing it. If the employee isn't really supposed to do this task in his or her job responsibility, but several employees have in the past, we should be careful before we do much training. Training is time consuming, and that means money. For this reason, we not only train to get results, but we are careful in selecting the methods that are used for training.

## DISCUSSION QUESTIONS

1. Why do we train? List both invalid and valid reasons.
2. What are the advantages of training over "throwing

them in over their heads and letting them learn to swim?"

3. What is the basic rule in training?

4. List specific steps in accomplishing successful training.

5. How important is follow-up after the initial training and how can we accomplish this?

## chapter ten

# Assessing Our Own Potential

Now comes the hard part. We've talked a lot about what supervisors do and what we can do to get ready to be a supervisor. At some point in time we have to take a long, hard look at ourselves and decide just what our strengths and weaknesses are. It is called "introspection." It isn't easy. We usually aren't very accurate. We can do a good job of appraising how well we are doing on our *present* job, but it's difficult to get a feel for how well we would do on another job, unlike our present job. No matter what our job is now, becoming a supervisor isn't going to be like it. We have to try, though, to figure out how good we will be, and what our shortcomings and strengths are, so we can be preparing ourselves to be ready when the time comes. In the next chapter we talk about getting ready for that job. In this chapter we talk about finding out what we can do well and what we need to improve upon. We'll not only see how to determine these things but how to use the information to our advantage.

# DETERMINING OUR STRENGTHS

How good are we? Is it bad to ask this kind of question? No, not if we expect to grow into a better job. Interestingly, when we find out how good we are, we also find out how bad we are! We don't limit ourselves to just the things we do well. We have to get a profile of our total self, all our good and bad job qualities. How do we do it? Well, we constantly go back and measure our performance as compared to what we should have done. We look at how well we did a job, how fast we did the job, how well what we did matched up with what was expected of us, and we get a good picture of our *present* worth. But we need to know our potential, not just what we're able to do right now. We often hear people say, "I think I'd be good at a supervisory job." How do they know? Is it intuition or do they have real evidence? It's good to imagine what great things we will do, but in the real world, we have to perform to standards, as we've seen, so fantasy won't help.

What evidence is there that we will be able to communicate well with people? The evidence is that we see good signs that we are able to communicate well with people right now. We practice at being understood. We try to listen. We measure our accuracy at listening and at getting the message across the first time. What evidence is there that we will be able to motivate people? It is that we see in ourselves the results of getting responsibility and what happens when we get certain needs met. We feel we'll be able to transfer this to others when the time comes. What evidence is there that we'll be able to delegate well? We see how delegation is done by others, and we see in our own job times when we would have liked to have more things delegated to us. What are the signs that we will be good at appraising employees? We look at the employees we work with and we find that we're able to determine their strengths and weaknesses. We match skills with our supervisor—in our own minds—to see how he or she rates an employee, and decide that we have some skill in these areas.

As we look at the things supervisors do, which we find out about by reading books like this and from observing supervisors at work, we work hard at determining how good we are at each of the skills. Right now we're talking about skills that we're good at, *our strengths*, in other words. We experiment a little with delegating, appraising, training, communicating, and the other skills, and we catalog our strengths. We conclude that there are some things we will be good at. So, what good does this do for us? We'll soon see that it will do us a lot of good, not only in preparing to be a supervisor, but in getting there more quickly!

So far we've talked only about skills that we *now* have to some degree. This is more of a self-appraisal than it is assessing our *potential*. Somehow we have to figure out what we will be good at in the years to come. We need to know what our potential is. We have to look at our present skill level and decide if we've grown as far as we can in certain areas, or if there is still a possibility that we can be even better than we are now at some things. In fact, as we look at the skills that supervisors will need, we realize that there are several that we'll never get a chance to practice very much, so we can't watch ourselves and decide if we're good or bad. What do we do then? Do we just guess, or leave it up to chance by tossing a coin and saying "Heads I'm good, tails I'm bad?" Obviously not, so what do we do?

Many people who have become good supervisors found out their potential by substituting themselves for the bosses around them (mentally) and matching wits with them— *without their bosses ever knowing it.* If they were wondering about their skill at problem solving or decision making, these would-be supervisors would see a problem arise, know that some decision was going to be made by the supervisor, and would treat the problem as if it were their own. They would determine the real problem to be solved, think of alternatives, consider the consequences of each of the possible solutions, then in their minds decide what they thought should be done. When the real supervisor finally made a decision or solved the problem, they would match theirs with that of the supervisor and see how well they did. If there was a difference, often they would check with that supervisor and see why the decision was made the way it was. It wasn't a matter of challenging the supervisor's decision. They just listened and gained from the experience. One thing they almost always learned was that in most cases the difference arose from one of two causes: Either they didn't have all the information, or they found that there was more than one satisfactory solution, maybe including their own. Throughout this book we've mentioned ways of watching other people, including supervisors, at work, constantly checking ourselves against the thoughts and actions of others, whether it be problem solving, decision making, appraising, or any other of the many skills supervisors need to be good in. We can assess our own potential by measuring ourselves against others doing these things, then decide how well we would have done, and how we can improve ourselves.

## USING OUR STRENGTHS

We've already seen that we can find out our strengths if we really want to know them. What do we do with them after we know what they are? Like any skill, we not only can improve them by using them, but especially by using them in our present jobs. This is easy to do. The important thing is to use them purposefully by writing a good memo or making a good presentation to the boss on a particular problem. Think about it ahead of time. Figure out ways of making the presentation better or plan on ways of getting feedback. If we have information to share with somebody —the boss or a co-worker—we should say to ourselves, "This is a good time for us to check on our communications skills," then build in feedback processes, check our listening skills, and decide when it's over if we used the skill well. If we feel that we did well, then we can check it off as a skill we're holding our own on, but if we feel it wasn't handled very well, we may try to find out what went wrong. Instead of just shrugging our shoulders and forgetting about it, we try to make a learning experience out of it.

There is another reason for using our strengths, of course. If anybody is ever going to be impressed with us, it's going to be because they've seen us perform well at something. We will not get a supervisory job because somebody thinks we can do the job, but has never seen us doing things well. We use our strengths as a means of demonstrating our capability and our potentials, too. We'll talk about letting our strengths be known to others later in this and the following chapter, so let's just leave it for now with the admonition that it's a lot easier for people to make decisions about us when they've actually seen us in action, doing something well, than if they have to use their imagination to determine how we will be able to perform in another job.

## OVERCOMING BAD IMAGES

No matter how well we have done our jobs and no matter what kind of strengths we have at the present time, very few of us have been around for long without getting crossways with somebody in the organization, or without blundering in one way or another in our jobs. When this happens, we find that it can blemish our record or leave a bad impression in people's minds. Some people have a bad image of us. Even though our performance may improve in this very area, there are still those who remember the poor performance or the times when our attitude wasn't what it should have been. We would like to think it wouldn't affect our chances for promotion, but we have to admit that it can and often does affect it. What can we do to overcome this? Are we stuck with the bad image or can we hope to overcome the image with those people who feel as they do about us? There are some things we can do that will help and we should start on them immediately if we expect to clear up the mistakes we've made.

First, we have to admit that we haven't always been perfect. This isn't something that we're forced to do even if we've been perfect; for most of us, however, it's a matter of simply looking back on events and deciding that there were times when we didn't use good judgment, our attitude was slipping, we had a personality conflict with a certain supervisor, or we just plain blundered. There might have been times in our career when we were unhappy and it affected our performance or when we just didn't perform very well for whatever the reason, but now we can begin to overcome some of the damage that may have been done.

After we've admitted that such things did occur, we decide who might have been around and unfavorably influenced by our performance at that time. Who was our supervisor? Who did we cross swords with? Who got their feelings hurt or might have been disappointed in us? Who depended on us, only to have a project fall through or be late or end up unsatisfactorily? We can usually answer most of these questions. These people may not have been unhappy at the time or for that matter may not remember our

"Fred, is this you in the 'Dear Evie' column? 'Dear Evie, What can I do? — I've discovered my only strength is that I recognize all my weaknesses.'"

performance at that time, but we can figure out who they are just the same. We know who was around at the time, and these are the first people we should begin to influence.

It's not a matter of going out of our way to look good in front of these particular people, but it is close. It wouldn't hurt us if we made a list of "possible suspects" and made sure that our performance is not only very satisfactory in front of them, but that they know that we are willing to adjust our performance to be better if they feel there is need for our improving. We aren't talking about some sort of under-handed process where we try to fool somebody into think-ing we're someone we really aren't. What we are trying to do is overcome an image we got by performing poorly. The way we are going to do this is by performing well in front of these same people. The only thing we aren't going to do is go up to them and say, "I know you think I'm a lousy em-ployee, so I'm going to show you that you're wrong." What we're going to hope for is that they will see us performing well, and say to themselves (and hopefully others), "Say, I guess I was wrong about them. I remembered them as hav-ing not been so good, but now that I have seen them per-form on this task, I've changed my mind."

There's a disappointing note that we have to admit about all of this. Unfortunately, *it usually takes a longer time and better work to change people's minds than it does to get their minds set in the first place.* We can get a bad image with one wrong deed, or by making a mistake one time on an important job, but doing one thing right won't necessar-ily get us back in the good graces of these people. They'll want to see us doing well on all of our assignments over a period of time, in order to be convinced that we are capa-ble of doing a satisfactory job. This may seen unfair, but it is human nature. When we blundered, it may have been in a situation where much was at stake. Because of our error, it made a lasting impression on the people involved. No wonder that it will take some good, prolonged performance on our part—in situations that aren't critical or as impressive —to change our image.

Another thing we can do to improve our image with the people we feel have been unfavorably impressed with us, is to let them see that our attitudes have changed. Many try to do this by running around and "polishing the apple" with these people. There is a much more mature way of doing it. We can be prepared to discuss the business or the job at hand in a knowledgeable way with them, without overdoing it. People are always pleasantly surprised when employees can discuss the job in an intelligent way. This will make an immediate impression on them, and in most cases a lasting one. The skill is to be certain we really do know what we're talking about, rather than launching into a discussion of some intricate accounting procedure about which we know only a few words. The safest way to do this is to stick with our job and talk about it. We can get into the conversation by asking questions. We might ask for some ideas of what the future looks like in this area, or if there seems to be any ideas about mechanizing or streamlining the operation. If we've done any reading or studying or talking with experts about it, we might share that; again remember not to snow the person under with gobbledygook, but make a short, intelligent conversation aimed at letting the person know that we really care about the job. If the person wants to extend the conversation, fine. If we run out of information, we'll do well to admit our lack of knowledge in the area of discussion and show an interest in improving our skill. *This is best done by being a good listener, rather than a good talker.*

We ought to realize several things about this problem. First, we don't want to overdo image-improving, it can quickly become obnoxious if we aren't careful, and we'll end up doing more harm than good. Next, we have to realize that doing a good, everyday kind of job should improve our image, so the important thing is to make sure our present job is done with as good an attitude and performance as possible. Finally, we must remember that others whom we know nothing about may have gotten a bad impression of us, perhaps from talking to those who saw us, or knew us "back when." In the case of these people, we'll have to depend on our good reputation spreading in the same manner as the poor image, by those who know our attitudes and actions.

## DETERMINING OUR WEAKNESSES

So far, we've talked about how to determine our strengths and how to use them to our advantage. It is important that we also get a good picture of our weaknesses. We need to know where to improve and where to exercise our strengths to overcome our weaknesses. How do we find out about our weaknesses? The same way we found out about our strengths, of course. Interestingly enough, finding out our faults is usually easier than finding out our strong points. When we think about it, we'll see that it's natural, since we are quickly informed when we do a job incorrectly, while doing it correctly may not elicit any comment. (We would do well to remember this when we become supervisors. People need to know what they're doing well as much as they need to know when they're not meeting standards.)

There are specific times when we get information on our performance, and this includes our strengths and weaknesses. Appraisal time is the most obvious time when we should listen and gather information. Here is an opportunity for us to be told by our immediate supervisor exactly how we are being perceived by those that work over us. What better way could we ask for finding out where we have skills already developed and where we have some work to do! When we've been doing an operation or task for some time and complete it, we may get some kind of review from our boss. If not, it's a good time to ask, "How'd I do?" Ask for a review, and make it clear that the purpose isn't to receive laurels, but to acquire information on good and/or bad performance. Even when we're ready to start a new project, we can use this as a time to ask for guidance as to areas where we might have problems (our weaknesses) and where we are expected to perform without guidance (our strengths).

# OVERCOMING OUR WEAKNESSES

Just as we need to use the information about our strengths to advantage, we also should use the information on our weaknesses to our advantage. This simply means that we should start immediately, on finding out about a weakness, to overcome it. We can't afford to be resentful when somebody tells us there is something we aren't doing as well as we should. Anytime somebody tells us something we need improvement on, we should be thankful for it, and regard it as a favor, not merely a criticism. We can make a mistake, though, if we don't let these same people help us improve. When our boss, for instance, points out a failure on our part, the best thing possible for us to do is to ask for help and advice on improving in that work area or skill.

Whatever advice we receive should be followed, if at all possible. We're getting good assistance from somebody who knows our work well, so it stands to reason that the advice should be good. Not only should we use this help in improving, but we should also ask for a follow-up evaluation after we've tried some suggestions. In fact, at the time we ask for suggestions for improvements, we can ask for a review. By simply saying, "Could we go over this again in a couple of weeks," we've opened the door for getting this "spot" off of our image. If nothing else, this will give us an incentive to improve or overcome this identified weakness.

# STAYING HONEST WITH OURSELVES

The theme of this chapter is assessing our own potential. We've tried to show ways of finding and dealing with our strengths and weaknesses. The problem we often have, though, is that we aren't completely honest with ourselves when we get down to the point where we either do something about the weakness or we need to use the strengths. We are biased about our own abilities. We either lose heart and decide that we aren't as good as we think we are, or we fool ourselves into thinking that we really aren't as bad in a certain area as people would have us believe. Sticking our heads in the sand is foolish and dangerous to our career. *We have to know how well we're doing*, in order to go on from there. If there were ever a time when we need to look into a clean mirror, it's when we want to get a good image of ourselves.

If somebody shows us that we're weak in doing a certain kind of job, we should believe it first—especially if there is obvious supporting data—and only stop believing it when the data no longer supports the idea. One thing that will help us believe it is to realize that if somebody thinks we are not as good in our performance as they would like to see, there must be a reason for their thinking that way, even if it's not true! Something in our actions gave them this impression, so if nothing else, we should examine our actions to see what is so misleading about them. There's no advantage in looking the other way, or in hearing just the good things. And, we should be equally honest when we hear good things said about us. If we hear somebody say that we've done something well, and we know that we were lucky to get out without the project falling apart, we need to realize this and not hide behind the compliment. Self-deception is easy. Facing the truth can be painful. Improving our performance requires that we suffer a little pain along with the joy of doing the job.

## CONCLUSION

In order to grow as we should to the job of supervisor, we have to know how well we're doing, and what our potential looks like. Finding out these things isn't easy or always satisfying, but it is essential. We need to know what we do well, and what we do poorly. Things we do well now will allow us to establish a reputation for possible accomplishments in the future. Things we do not do well will give us something to work on in trying to prepare for our future as a supervisor. We have to face up to our weaknesses, even those that we had in the past that we've overcome now. They will continue to haunt us, if we aren't careful. We can use our strengths to overcome bad images, and we can improve our weaknesses by dealing directly with them, rather than by refusing to admit that they exist. If we react properly when we find out about a shortcoming, we can use that as an opportunity to seek advice on improvement. If we play the role right, we can even get it off of our record by having a specified review time to look at our efforts at improvement. What we really want to know is how good we will be in the future when we're doing things that are different from what we're doing now. No one can tell us that, but if we stay honest with ourselves, we can make some educated predictions. We hope our present performance will show others that they, too, can depend on us in their predictions!

## DISCUSSION QUESTIONS

1. Make a list of your strengths. Think of ways you can use each of them, both in your current job and in the future.

2. Make a list of your weaknesses. Consider ways of overcoming them.

3. A good way to assess our potential is by measuring ourselves against others. Pick a boss, substitute yourself (mentally) for him or her and match wits with this boss without his or her knowledge. How do you measure up?

4. How can we overcome bad images in the workplace?

## chapter eleven

# Preparing for the Supervisory Role

So far we've talked mostly about the *skills* needed to be a supervisor. We haven't said much about the *attitude* required in preparation for the job. To be effective, we're not only going to have to think like a supervisor when we become one, but we're going to have to do the right kind of thinking between now and then. This last chapter will deal with the proper frame of mind needed to prepare ourselves and to endure until that time. We use the term endure advisedly, since there are going to be times when that's what we'll be doing. As we develop the skills, we may see those already at supervisory level who don't seem to be doing as well at it as we think we could. We will have to endure. We will see others around us get promoted before us, when we think we could and should get the job instead of them. We will have to endure. Our own supervisor may not be helping us in the ways we have suggested in this book, thereby perhaps delaying our promotion. Again, we will endure. Let's see what we're preparing for, and how we can prepare.

# GETTING READY FOR WHAT?

One of these days, perhaps when we are least expecting it, someone will inform us that we have just been selected to take over a supervisory role, starting next Monday. Today is Friday and we realize we have the weekend to get ready to be a supervisor. For all of our thinking about it, developing ourselves and preparing for it, we most likely will come close to a panic point for a few moments. We will begin to ask ourselves if we're really ready for the job. We'll wonder if we're big enough for the task. The thought will occur to us over the weekend that things are going to be different *from now on*. Whatever happens on Monday and the days to follow, will never place us back at this point again. Even if we (or the organization) decide we aren't the person for the job, we can never go back to being exactly who we are now.

So, we begin to get ready to be a supervisor. What are we getting ready for? What is a supervisor? There are many supervisors, and each seems to be doing a different job. How can we possibly get ready for one of these jobs when there are so many? These sound like good questions, but they aren't! They show a misunderstanding of the supervisor's job. Having come this far, we recognize that the job of a supervisor, any supervisor, involves getting the job done through other people. That's true if we're in the fields of accounting or construction, merchandising, sales, or production. That aspect of the work is always the same if the person is truly a supervisor.

What are we getting ready for? Some have called it the "lonely world." In many ways that's an accurate name for it. We have to give up some of our old alliances, some of our habits and some of our work. We won't be one of the gang anymore. People will be coming to us for help and advice and with complaints, and they'll be looking for answers and solutions. But thoughts like these are dangerous, because they make us begin to think that fun doesn't exist in the supervisory role, that there are no friends and no one to go to for help. Nothing could be further from the truth. It's a whole new, exciting world of work, with tremendous challenges and fantastic personal rewards. If we can't think in these terms then we have no place in the ranks of supervision.

# BEING MENTALLY PREPARED

We have to begin to get our minds in order right now so we'll be prepared for the job when it comes. First, we have to be prepared for the wait, the time between now and then. If we spend that time observing, as we've suggested throughout this book, we can make this waiting profitable. We can psych ourselves up or down, depending entirely on how we approach ourselves in our present job. Certainly we will get frustrated and even disillusioned over many things, as we've already said, but if we let that get to us, then we're probably demonstrating that we aren't ready to be a supervisor. Not many things that frustrate us now will be worse than what we will face as a supervisor. When we get home at night and want to kick our dog, scream at our spouse, and threaten the kids with mayhem, perhaps we can even learn to smile a little and say, "Perhaps I'm getting a little presupervisory training!"

There's a statement somewhere that says that a good leader must be bigger than life. If we think of this as referring to our mental attitude, then it's a good statement. Ultimately, we will win the battle with our mental *approach*, rather than with our mental *skills*. If we can get our minds set right, then the thinking will take care of itself. Let's see what "setting right" is. First, it is developing a quiet kind of confidence that we can do the job we're going to be asked to do. How do we acquire confidence? By looking at others who are doing the same kind of work and deciding what skills they had when they first got the supervisory job. We'll usually find that they weren't any better at the tasks they were being asked to do than we are. We'll probably find that they had the same concerns that we have now.

Next, in getting our minds set correctly, we should forget, for a moment, that there is a difference between a supervisor and a nonsupervisor, as far as the organization is concerned. As we look at the jobs people are doing, the problems they're solving, the decisions they're making, we should ask ourselves, "Is what they're doing really that hard to do?" Most of the time the answer will be, "No, not really." This will bolster our confidence, but we have to be careful here, too. We can get overconfident. This can be avoided by convincing ourselves—properly so—that while the job isn't that hard, it is something that has to be learned, and can be done well or poorly, depending on how much training the supervisor has had. We will conclude that we can handle it once someone shows us how to do it.

The next thing we can do to get our minds set right is to realize that when the time comes that the organization thinks we can handle the job they will offer it to us, not before. This tells us several things. One, it says that we have those looking at us who know what supervisors do, and know basically what we can do. In the long run, they're probably a better judge than we are at deciding when there is a match between the requirements and our abilities. Another thing it tells us is that since they do know the job to be done and our abilities, then when they pick us for the supervisory role, we have no reason to think it is a bad decision. We can go into it with confidence. Finally, it tells us that there must still be some things we need to grow in, when we aren't chosen. Or, it may say that we haven't done our job of selling our strong points as well as we should.

Many who successfully make it to the supervisory ranks keep themselves in good mental shape by picking somebody removed from the mainstream of the organization and using them as a sounding board for their thoughts and ideas. Ideally, it is somebody who is experienced, positive toward the organization, and has a measure of success to show for the years put in, but does not control any part of the organization where the person aspiring to be a supervisor is working. It can even be somebody who is a supervisor in another organization entirely separate from the one we're in. We want to use such a person carefully, testing our thinking, getting advice, but *never* using it as an opportunity to complain or find fault with our organization. Developing such a working relationship with an experienced supervisor is invaluable if we pick the right person and use the information we acquire wisely.

# WHERE DO WE WANT TO BE?

It's sometimes dangerous for us to try to plot our own career. There is a difference between *plotting* a career and *planning one*. Let's see what the difference is. When we plan a career, we think in terms of where we are now, where we want to be, and then begin to plan those steps that we think will take us there. It means determining strengths and weaknesses as we've been talking about. It includes deciding what our best route is, that is, should we go back to school, change jobs in order to get on a better track, or continue in the same general direction. These are difficult decisions to make, and sometimes they end up being little more than guesses. But at least we've looked at the subjects we've mentioned, and we have made the decisions with the best information available to us at the time. The results are bound to be better than they would have been if we'd not looked at them at all. Even though we've made some guesses, we can begin to put together a good plan to achieve our goal. Our action is always based on as much information on hand as is available and is at least thought out in general terms. And that's the key: *general terms*. Our plan allows for changes and is modified as we go along. As we find out more about ourselves and what we can do, we make adjustments. Nothing is so rigid that we can't change it, whether it be direction, timing or the kind of work we'd like to be doing. We don't lock ourselves into a situation that we can't get out of, even though we are constantly trying to move ahead.

That's where plotting is different. Many people try to plot their careers right down to the time schedule when they will be at certain levels and doing specific things. This leaves no room for flexibility. There cannot be any turning back, or to the right or left. If they don't make this schedule, they consider themselves failures. Many times, they make it, of course. There are those who make a strong case for plotting a career. The trouble is that many people don't make it, and they end up frustrated and disappointed. There are those who make it, only to find out that they wish they had taken another route, or even waited awhile until things were clearer for them. Historically, we've always asked people in this country, "What do you want to be?" The implication is that everybody should have a specific goal readily available to answer that question. If we don't reply, "I want to be a supervisor in the shipping department within two years," we're seen as lacking ambition. If we answer, "I want to see how I fit into this organization and what my skills are before I set my sights on a specific job," we're seen as not very ambitious by some.

Perhaps the answer lies somewhere in between. There's no reason why we can't plan our career in a certain direction, based on the best information we have, but at the same time hedge a little on the exact date or even the exact job. As we look at those around us who have become a supervisor, for example, we can determine how long they had to wait, and what skills they had. We can match our service and skills with theirs and get an accurate idea of what our chances are. We can even project about when we can expect some kind of promotion. This is still planning, because we've reserved the right to change our minds. If we decide that we'd like to move ahead in the accounting department, and that means taking some courses in accounting at night, then we won't be disappointed if we have to wait a little longer than we originally planned. In fact, we may even discover ourselves trying to slow things down a little, so that we can get better prepared.

# WHEN DO WE WANT TO BE THERE?

Even though we may not have planned a specific time for making supervisor, we ought to have a general idea of where we're going and when we hope to be there. We've just talked about this. We need to think in terms of the organization, though, not just about ourselves. It may be that others have become a supervisor rather quickly, and we expect to do the same. This might not be the whole picture. Some may have made it because they had just the right skill at a time when that skill was needed. Others may have become one because the organization was expanding rapidly and many people were becoming supervisors with less than average service. Times change. Jobs get filled and then there is no movement. There may be cutbacks that mean that even those in supervisory jobs wonder if they'll be able to keep their positions. If our time comes along about then, we're obviously not going to make supervisor.

Nevertheless, after we've said all this about uncertainty, we still should be able to get a fairly good idea of when we can make a move upward. The easiest way is to look at the organization, the general rate of promotion, the number of people moving to other jobs or quitting, the competition for the jobs, and our own growth rate; and from all this set a target time. Once we know where we want to go, it's easier to decide when we want to get there. Do we change as the time gets closer? No, hopefully we won't have to because our habits will be good enough by then that most of what we do will be routine and well enough known that we won't have to make a big splash to be recognized. We need to do some checking, though, to be sure that we're moving as well as we should, that we've developed along the lines we planned and that we haven't left things undone that should have been accomplished.

The time we have set becomes critical for us, in other ways, too. If we approach the date (maybe the month or even the year of our promotion desire), we need to begin to make sure we have a positive mental attitude toward ourselves, the organization, and the work in general. It's easy for us to fall into a rut of complaining because everybody complains, or finding fault with working conditions, policies, or supervision. If we aren't careful, we'll follow the crowd in such things without realizing it. Before long, we develop a negative attitude, and it shows in our personality and in our work. The way to check ourselves is to go back to the beginning of this book and look at what we said about whom we'd look for if we were given the job of selecting a supervisor from the people around us. The simple question we would ask will give us most of the information we need about ourselves; Would we select *ourselves* for the job, if our work and attitude were like they were at that time? This is a brutal question for us to ask ourselves. Remember, we can't say, "Well, of course, I know myself well enough to know that I'd change if I got the job." That's not fair! Management has to accept us as we are *right now*, and assume that they're not going to get any more or any less from us than what we are showing at the time we are promoted.

# WHAT STANDS IN OUR WAY?

Now that we know where we want to go and when we want to get there, the obvious question is, "What stands in our way?" This requires more introspection. We have to look again at ourselves, what the shortcomings are that we discovered in our look for strengths and weaknesses, and decide which ones need to be overcome. Some we'll have to live with and work around. If we simply aren't mathematicians and no matter how hard we try we can't improve, we either learn a few shortcuts in accounting or stay out of the field altogether. If the job requires handling women, men, minorities, technical people, professionals, or older people —all in great numbers—and we are unable to work with these types of people without it bothering us, then we either decide to put in a tremendous effort to overcome it, or figure out another route.

Still we must not only look at our weaknesses; but, at the supervisors, the organization's policies and all of the things that are going on around us. We become very aware of what's happening. We familiarize ourselves with production and personnel requirements, and we make an effort to see what we can do to fit ourselves into that pattern of thinking. Not knowing these things is an obstacle and the lack of this knowledge stands in our way of becoming more important to the organization. So, we set a target of learning specific things within certain time frames. We decide that we will take an evening a week to study the service manual. We borrow a copy of the personnel manual—if one is available —and we study if *from a supervisor's point of view*. This is different from studying it with an idea of becoming a supervisor some day and having to use it. The lack of knowledge in these matters simply means that we can't *think* like a supervisor, so we can't get into the right frame of mind to act like one.

## AVOIDING ENTANGLEMENTS

If we are serious about becoming a supervisor some day, serious enough to go through the things suggested in this book, then we ought to avoid getting so involved in nonsupervisory things that we can't take the steps to improve ourselves or prepare our thoughts for the supervisory role. This doesn't mean that we can't participate in nonsupervisory activities or support employee groups. It simply means that we can't make that our whole life. We can't become so intense in changing the life of the nonsupervisory personnel that we forget that we want to be a part of the supervisory ranks ourselves. It might help us to think about what we can do *as supervisors* to change the lot of these people, rather than try to make all the changes come about before we get there. If we devote too much of our energies to this effort —fighting for employees rights—then we may get a much longer time to continue because we may lose our job while we're in the battle.

"Guess what? Mr. Slipshod called — you've been promoted to supervisor, starting tomorrow!"

Some feel that they might become a supervisor if they oppose the organization strongly enough to cause the organization to remove them from the nonsupervisory ranks just to get rid of them. This is a risky business, and for all that have made it this way, there are many more who haven't. These is perhaps a thin line between entangling ourselves in things that won't be conducive to getting us to the ranks of supervision and doing things that will help us develop our leadership ability. If we engage in employee activities, we ought to do it for several reasons. First, because we believe in the activity as a worthshile endeavor; second, because we think we can contribute something worthwhile to the endeavor; and third, because we think the activity will give us a chance to develop ourselves toward the goals we are striving for. There's a way to decide just how much we can expect to get out of the activity if we participate in it. We look at our role and decide if we're going to be leading or following. If we're leading, then there's a good chance we can practice many of our needed supervisory skills. It also suggests that we are taking some initiative in the matter, rather than just following somebody else's leadership in something we did not create and over which we have no control.

On the other hand, if we're simply following somebody, we won't exercise supervisory skills or receive much credit from management for demonstrating our skills along this line. As a follower, we'll be one of many, part of a large mass of people who are perhaps just going along with the crowd. There isn't much to be gained from this sort of activity.

Mostly we've been talking about activities that are organizationally oriented. There are other kinds of activities that can be harmful to us if we get too involved in them. Again, these are the kinds that are neither wrong nor harmful in themselves. It's what we do in them, what we can gain from them, and how they affect our present work that really count. For example, there are many outside activities, such as schoolwork, community projects, or children's sports activities, that need a lot of assistance from anyone who can help. As responsible citizens, we owe it to the community around us to give as much support as we possibly can. If every citizen took a fair share of the load, the work would go along smoothly and there would be much less for any one individual to do. But this isn't the case, so all of these activities are always looking for people who will devote large amounts of time to the work. If we're supervisory material, we most likely have a lot to offer. However, this can be our downfall. Too much time on the wrong activity can do us more harm than good.

When we set our sights on becoming a supervisor, we shouldn't give up outside activities, but we should put them in their proper perspective. We have to understand that anything that we do outside of work is all right, until it causes our job to suffer. If our doing it means that we can't work certain shifts and the organization has to work around us, then we aren't being fair to the organization. If it means that we have to spend time on the telephone during working hours or that we're too tired to think properly when we come in from long hours working with a committee for the local baseball club, then the job is suffering. We may be doing a great job for the outside activity, even learning some skills that would help us as supervisors, but if it's interfering with our job, we should devote less time to it. Remember, the organization usually wants us to be good citizens, but not at the expense of our work. We simply have to remember that the organization is paying us to get the job done. Anything else is extra.

What we've said about community projects and other worthwhile activities goes for second jobs as well—perhaps even more so. Many times we have opportunities, be-

cause of skills we have developed on the job or time schedules, to work at another job for several hours a week. We
enjoy the money, we don't have to do too much, and it
works out well for all concerned, until it starts to interfere
with our regular jobs for the reasons we just stated: interfering with schedules, causing fatigue, or taking away our interest. There are many people who never become a supervisor, and the main thing that kept them from becoming one
was a part-time job for which they received very little money
compared to what they missed by not getting the supervisory job. When management looked around for somebody,
these people were noted, but were seen as not being interested in a promotion, since they were putting a lot of time
into their second job. We can have other jobs, but it's up to
us to see that they don't keep us from reaching our planned
goal.

## HANDLING THE PRESENT JOB

Of all the things that are likely to get us promoted to supervisor, no one thing comes close to matching the importance of doing our present job well. There are very few
cases where anyone got promoted to a supervisory job,
who looked like they had potential, but were making mistakes on their present job. Many have made it to supervisor
and made mistakes on that job, but they were usually doing
well on the nonsupervisory job beforehand. We've talked
about many things we can do on our present jobs that will
give us practice for the supervisory job to follow. It's important that we use these opportunities when they arise. It's
more important, however, that we perform well at what
we're assigned to do on our present job.

There are those who have failed to make it to the next job

simply because they spend so much time worrying about a promotion that they made mistakes on their present job. We can and should avoid this at all cost. The process is simple. We find out what we're supposed to do, find out what the standard is for the expected performance, then do our best to meet or exceed this standard. This means one more step —finding out how we're doing. Listening when appraisal time comes around; reviewing with the boss at frequent intervals to keep ourselves informed on our progress—especially in those areas where we've been told that we have shortcomings.

There are two ways to draw attention to ourselves. One is to do such a bad job that we're being watched constantly. The other is to do such a good job that we draw attention from the people over us who are looking for people who can get the job done. The first one will almost always get us more attention than the second and more immediately. It's the kind we'd rather not have, of course, and yet it seems sometimes that no matter how good we are, nobody notices. Just let us blunder and we will receive more than our share of attention. There is some consolation in the fact that we are slower in getting attention from doing well than from doing poorly. At least we finally do get some, when we do an exceptionally fine job. If we just do a mediocre job— neither good nor bad—then *we don't receive any attention at all.*

# MAKING OUR OWN LUCK

We've saved the subject of luck until the end. There are those who say that no matter how hard we try and no matter how hard we work, the fact is that luck gets us about as many breaks as the hard work. We'll have to admit that there is something to be said for that. Luck does play an important part in our success. Some people seem to be in the right place at the right time. They seem to be talking to the right person when an opportunity comes up or they're on a particular assignment when that one becomes important. They seem to be lucky enough that they've just finished a very satisfactory appraisal of themselves by their bosses when an opening comes up and they get it. So why should we worry about planning or even about practicing all these skills if luck is going to play the deciding hand? If we feel that way, we don't understand luck!

The secret to luck, as far as getting ahead in the organization, is that we usually *make our own luck*. If we practiced all the things we've talked about in this book—learning from watching others, pairing our appraisals with those of the boss, asking about the future of the organization, finding out where the emphasis is going to be in the weeks and months ahead, getting an overview of the business, keeping abreast of our own job and our ratings in that job—we're going to be in the right place at the right time, talking to the right people, doing the right job. We're going to be there because our performance will have caused it! Luck will play an important part, but it will be luck that we helped to manufacture *all by ourselves*.

## CONCLUSION

In this chapter we've seen that after we've done all of the things mentioned in this book, we also have to get our mind in working order. We must put our mind in positive gear. We have to learn patience. It will help us to plan—not plot—where we'd like to be and when we'd like to be there, though this needs to have some flexibility built into it. We have to know our own weaknesses, since they may be in our way of getting where we want to go. We have to decide what else is in our way, and see what it will take to get them out of the way. We need to put our own job first, ahead of outside activities, ahead of getting the next job, ahead of anything that will keep us from making our own luck by performing well in that job. We can make it to the supervisory ranks if we want to get there, but the key person needed to get us there is our own self. That's the only person who can get us there, no matter what others may try to do for us. *Our own performance will be the key factor in whatever success we have.*

# DISCUSSION QUESTIONS

1.  How can we begin to prepare for the job of supervisor?

2.  What is the difference in "plotting" a career and "planning" one?

3.  Is it possible to predict not only where we are going, but when we want to be there?

4.  What are some disadvantages of becoming over involved in nonsupervisory activities?

5.  Of all the things that are likely to get us promoted to supervisor, which is the most important?

6.  What part does "luck" play in getting us ahead in the organization?

# Epilogue

No one is ever going to be made a supervisor just because they read a book! Not even this book. Reading this book hopefully will not harm you, and may *help* you get ready to be a supervisor, but it won't do it all. It certainly won't make you the supervisor you want to be. What will? Time, practice, experience, self-analysis, self-development, and a great deal of self-made luck. Looking at those who have made it to the supervisory ranks shows that they are the ones who not only *aspired* to the job, but *perspired* to get there, too. Some don't like it after they've been promoted. The majority do, because of the challenge and the reward that go with it. But getting there is up to you. It may sound trite, but it's true: You, more than anyone else, will determine whether or not you make it to supervisor. Good luck, and good supervising!

# appendices

# Five Self-Evaluation Devices

In this section we've placed a few things that will provide more information on how to act as a supervisor. More than anything, we've tried to give something that we can use to test ourselves against those who are presently succeeding as supervisors. Five items are included. Three are charts that show step-by-step actions in getting a particular job done. The last two are lists of characteristics shown by successful supervisors as they carry out two important functions of supervision—neither of which was included in the book, since they really don't qualify as "survival" skills.

# Simple Steps in Problem Solving

Almost everything a supervisor does is somehow related to problem solving. We haven't included a separate chapter in the main text, because to become a good problem solver takes a lot of practice and assistance. In most reading material on the subject, the following steps will be shown in one form or another. We've included it so that the reader can get a feel for the steps, and perhaps even practice them on some problems.

# Simple Steps in Problem Solving

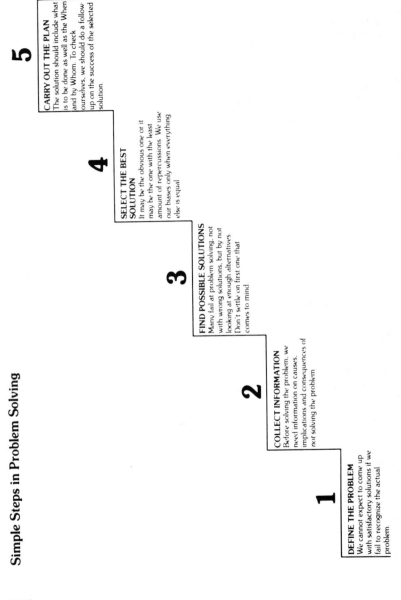

**1**

**DEFINE THE PROBLEM**
We cannot expect to come up with satisfactory solutions if we fail to recognize the actual problem

**2**

**COLLECT INFORMATION**
Before solving the problem, we need information on causes, implications and consequences of *not* solving the problem

**3**

**FIND POSSIBLE SOLUTIONS**
Many fail at problem solving, not with wrong solutions, but by not looking at enough alternatives Don't settle on first one that comes to mind

**4**

**SELECT THE BEST SOLUTION**
It may be the obvious one or it may be the one with the least amount of repercussions We use our biases only when everything else is equal

**5**

**CARRY OUT THE PLAN**
The solution should include what is to be done as well as the When and by Whom To check ourselves, we should do a follow-up on the success of the selected solution

# The Communications Cycle

Communicating isn't something we do separately and apart from the job. For the most part, it *is* the job of a supervisor. We communicate up, down, and across in the organization. This chart and the information on it will help the reader to understand why we call it complex. Hopefully, it will also remove some of the confusion.

# The Communications Cycle

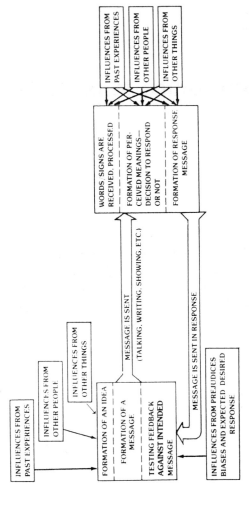

INFLUENCES FROM PAST EXPERIENCES

INFLUENCES FROM OTHER PEOPLE

INFLUENCES FROM OTHER THINGS

FORMATION OF AN IDEA

FORMATION OF A MESSAGE

TESTING FEEDBACK AGAINST INTENDED MESSAGE

MESSAGE IS SENT
(TALKING, WRITING, SHOWING, ETC.)

INFLUENCES FROM PREJUDICES BIASES AND EXPECTED DESIRED RESPONSE

MESSAGE IS SENT IN RESPONSE

WORDS, SIGNS ARE RECEIVED, PROCESSED

FORMATION OF PER-CEIVED MEANINGS—DECISION TO RESPOND OR NOT

FORMATION OF RESPONSE MESSAGE

INFLUENCES FROM PAST EXPERIENCES

INFLUENCES FROM OTHER PEOPLE

INFLUENCES FROM OTHER THINGS

**NOTE:** Communicating is a complex process. The above chart represents only one-half of the cycle: The sender formulates an idea, then sends a message by some process. The message is received by the receiver, and some meaning is attached to it. If a response is deemed necessary by the receiver, it is sent. This only represents the action of the original sender and the receiver. The whole process is repeated if the receiver becomes a sender with a new contribution rather than a response. Note that both are constantly influenced by people, situations and past experiences.

218

# Steps in Successful Training

This flow chart provides the reader with the key ingredients to getting the training job done. For training to be satisfactory it must include all of these steps and the information contained in them.

# Steps in Successful Training

**INPUTS:**

**TRAINEE:** Capable of doing the job; well prepared mentally for training; sees training as an opportunity, not a chore; eager to learn new skill.

**TRAINER:** Has knowledge of the skill to be taught; knows how to train; sees training as an obligation, not a service; wants employee to learn.

**SKILL:** Well defined; standards have been set and are measurable.

**GOAL:** Known by trainer and the trainee; includes acceptable and expected outcomes of the training.

**TRAINING:**

**TRAINING:** Gets the trainee involved; provides for frequent interaction of trainee and trainer; allows both learner and trainer to get feedback on progress of learning; is flexible enough to allow better learner access to skill; provides opportunities for trainee to discover important concepts about the skill being learned.

**OUTPUTS:**

**TRAINEE:** Goals are met and demonstrated during the training; trainee knows that learning has taken place; learner wants to try new skills in the job situation.

**TRAINER:** Checks training effort against trainee skills; evaluates training in terms of use of skills on the job; follows up on training effort to see how much modification is needed in the training approach.

# Characteristics of Good Discipline

Any supervisor is going to have to exercise discipline at one time or another. Those who are successful at it offer this set of characteristics for those who want to do it well. We offer them to the reader as a guide. Someday they may make the difference in success or failure as a disciplinarian.

*Characteristics of Good Discipline*

1. *Fair.* Fairness is sometimes hard to determine, but in discipline it means applying the same rules to everybody, and applying the same consequences to violators, regardless of the people involved.

2. *Without Emotion.* Avoid applying disciplinary action when we are at a high pitch of emotion. Our judgment isn't as good during these times and we're likely to do or say something we'll regret. Ideally, we should learn to control our emotions rather than keep delaying discipline.

3.  *Timely.* The discipline should come as close to the violation as possible, so the employees will relate the two.

4.  *Without Surprise.* There should be a thorough understanding of the reasons for the discipline. The consequences for breaking the rules ought to be explained and understood before disciplinary action is taken, not while it is going on.

5.  *Avoid Threats.* Discipline is the result of a failure on the part of the employee, the boss, or both. It should not be viewed as a means of "getting at" somebody. We should never offer a consequence for an action if we aren't willing or able to carry out that consequence.

6.  *Documented.* We should feel that documenting employee actions—especially where violations of rules or policies are concerned—is an essential part of the supervisors job. Avoiding the trouble of paperwork and employee discussion required by documentation of the actions, is a step away from successful supervision.

7.  *Discipline for Improvement.* The purpose of discipline is either for prevention or correction. Early discipline, when the first infractions occur, can prevent later violations by an employee as well as by others who observe the discipline take place. It should always be viewed as a means to *improve* the situation, not just preserve it.

# Characteristics of Successful Supervisors

Finally, we've included a self-test and a list of things that we will have to be good at before becoming successful as supervisors. As is pointed out on the list, this isn't complete, but if we possess a high degree of all of these characteristics, we'll be up with some of the best!

*Characteristics of Successful Supervisors*

NOTE: Trying to find characteristics that successful supervisors have in common is difficult. The following list is a collection of characteristics and traits that seem to be common to all who have shown a high degree of success at supervision. It isn't exhaustive, but it offers a good target for all of us.

1. *Willingness to Work.* This doesn't mean we cannot stop working or that we are workaholics. It means that when there is work to be done right away, we can't rest easy until it's finished. A good deal of patience is required, because not all of the people

around us will respond to the challenge, and we may end up doing the subordinate's work.

2. *Willingness to Take Risks.* Successful supervisors have seen that the taking of responsibility automatically results in certain risks. Often the stakes are high: reward for success, unpleasantness for failure. The successful supervisor weighs the consequences, determines the skills required, then attacks the problem if the chances for success are reasonable.

3. *Enthusiasm.* The best enthusiasm is the kind that comes with getting a job done well. Successful supervisors are enthusiastic about new approaches, or about getting the job done quickly or more efficiently. Such enthusiasm is invariably catching!

4. *Empathetic.* Empathy is knowing what it's like to be in the other person's shoes, whether it's the bosses', a peer's or a subordinate's. The successful supervisor uses empathy to decide the proper approach to take with different people in different situations. This is basically a matter of understanding why people act the way they do, and using this information to get the job done.

5. *Ability to Motivate.* Allowing employees to be responsible for something, or to have a chance to achieve or get recognition, results in internal motivation, which is the best kind. Sometimes external motivation is necessary, which is when employees work because of us instead of the job. Ideally, we should use the job to motivate the employees, since that way they are more likely to work whether we're there or not.

6. *Ability to Communicate.* Successful communicators know what they want to say, and then know that the message was received. They use feedback

—mostly listening skills—to determine if it was received in the form they sent it in. They know when a message is *misunderstood*, as well as when it's understood.

# Index